TWAYNE'S WORLD AUTHORS SERIES

A Survey of the World's Literature

Sylvia E. Bowman, Indiana University

GENERAL EDITOR

ITALY

Carlo Golino, University of Massachusetts at Boston

EDITOR

Lorenzo de'Medici

(TWAS 288)

Lorenzo de'Medici

Lorenzo de'Medici

By SARA STURM

University of Massachusetts

Twayne Publishers, Inc.   ::   New York

Library of Congress Cataloging in Publication Data

Sturm, Sara.
   Lorenzo de'Medici.

   (Twayne's world authors series, TWAS 288. Italy)
   Bibliography: p. 167
   1. Medici, Lorenzo de', il Magnifico, 1449–1492.
 PQ4630.M3Z87   851'.2   73-19597
 ISBN 0–8057–2609–8

For Mark and Jeffrey

Preface

In presenting Lorenzo de'Medici as a literary figure, one has the unusual disadvantage of discussing a man who is too well known. He was the most important citizen of Florence in what is generally considered that city's most important hour; the historian Francesco Guicciardini was to write of Lorenzo and of his grandfather Cosimo that "both were so eminent in virtue and fortune that perhaps since the fall of Rome Italy has had no private citizen to be compared with them."[1] As that age known to us as the Renaissance flourished in Florence, Lorenzo was both a leader in its principal events and a singularly faithful mirror of its major intellectual movements. His figure imposes itself so clearly on any study of the Renaissance that he has been called "the protagonist of the new age."[2]

It is unfortunate that this very prominence has obscured his genuine literary achievement. Many studies of the man make only passing mention of his poetry. Even studies devoted to Florentine Renaissance literature sometimes consider Lorenzo in this context only as patron, acknowledging his contribution in encouraging the works of such writers as Pulci and Poliziano, but summarily dismissing his own poetry as politically motivated or as the amusement of a restless dilettante. While Lorenzo took himself seriously as a poet, historians and critics have been reluctant to do so, and the limited treatment accorded his literary work has frequently assumed the nature of controversy, even of polemic. Yet Lorenzo the poet was not of lesser stature or lesser importance to his period than Lorenzo the patron or statesman; if he had not distinguished himself as the outstanding statesman of the Italian Renaissance, he would have been remembered as one of its greatest poets.

The present volume attempts the difficult but necessary task of removing Lorenzo's poetry from the shadow of his fame as man of action, in order to survey his achievement as man of letters. Because not all of those for whom this volume is intended may read the original texts with ease, and because in some cases useful translations into English are not currently available, the substance of the works is fully presented. Detailed reference to Lorenzo's activity as statesman and patron, to which a growing number of readily accessible studies are devoted, is not possible within the scope of this volume, nor is it possible here to consider in detail the problems of attribution and chronology which make the study of his poetry particularly difficult. Rather than attempt a presentation according to a tentative and disputed chronology, this volume takes as its point of departure that variety in Lorenzo's work which has proved so disconcerting to critics, discussing the poems in terms of their dominant sources: his own observation of life in his native Tuscany, the Italian vernacular tradition of love-poetry, the classical influence, and religious and philosophical questions.

While questions raised by the various works are suggested and some new appraisals of the poetry are offered, the primary aim of this volume is to serve as a brief critical introduction, to make Lorenzo's literary work as a whole accessible to the English-reading public.

SARA STURM

University of Massachusetts

Contents

Chronology

1449 January 1, Lorenzo de'Medici born, in Florence, to Piero di Cosimo de'Medici and Lucrezia Tornabuoni.

1459 Takes part in public procession in honor of Galeazzo Maria Sforza's visit to Florence.

1464 His grandfather Cosimo dies; his father, Piero, assumes charge of the affairs of Florence.

1465 Represents the Medici at the marriage in Milan of Ippolita Sforza and Alfonso of Aragon, the Duke of Calabria.

1466 Visits Ferdinand of Aragon in Naples; begins active participation in public affairs in Florence.

1469 February 7, Lorenzo is awarded first place in a tourney in honor of Lucrezia Donati; June 4, he marries Clarice Orsini; December 2, his father dies, and two days later he accepts the charge of head of the Florentine state.

1471 Birth of his first child, Piero; attends the coronation of Pope Sixtus IV in Rome.

1472 Provides for the reopening of the University of Pisa; Volterra revolts against Florence, and is sacked by mercenary troops.

1474 Beginning of hostilities between Lorenzo and Pope Sixtus IV; establishment of the alliance between Milan, Venice, and Florence.

1478 The Conspiracy of the Pazzi results in the death of Lorenzo's brother, Giuliano, and in the consolidation of Lorenzo's own power in Florence. The Pope places the city under an interdiction and enlists the aid of the king of Naples against Florence.

1480 Lorenzo's bold visit to King Ferdinand in Naples achieves an accord; at the end of the year, the Pope lifts the interdiction against Florence.

1481 A second conspiracy against Lorenzo is discovered and punished.

1482 His mother, Lucrezia, dies.

1484 Peace is concluded; Pico della Mirandola arrives in Florence.

1486 Lorenzo attains preeminence in Italian affairs through his role in negotiations after the "Barons' War" with the new Pope Innocent VIII.

1488   His daughter Maddalena is married to Franceschetto Cibo, son of Innocent VIII; his wife Clarice dies.

1489   Savonarola is recalled to Florence.

1490   Lorenzo concerns himself with the acquisition of a great library, aided by Pico and Poliziano.

1492   His son, Giovanni, the future Pope Leo X, is officially named cardinal. On April 8, Lorenzo dies at Careggi.

It is not possible to present a reliable chronology of Lorenzo's literary works. Very few dates have been established with certainty, despite the continuing efforts of a number of scholars.

CHAPTER 1

Protagonist of the New Age

WHEN Lorenzo de'Medici was born, on the first day of the year 1449, the city of Florence was a center of intense cultural and intellectual activity. Following the achievements of Dante, Petrarch, and Boccaccio in the fourteenth century, Florence had maintained the initiative in the advancement of learning and in the arts, and near the turn of the century the "first great flowering" of humanism had its focus there.[1] In 1402, the city had been victorious in her defense of republican independence against Milan, and the civic fervor occasioned by the conflict combined with the new humanist interpretations of Florentine history to produce a conviction of living in a new age of greatness. This view, which sometimes found expression in a sense of cultural mission, dominated the development of Florentine thought during the first half of the fifteenth century.[2] Marsilio Ficino, the city's leading philosopher during the second half of the century, struck a popular note when he exclaimed that "this is a golden age, one which has restored to prominence the liberal disciplines which were almost extinguished: grammar, poetry, eloquence, painting, architecture, sculpture, music, the art of singing to the ancient lyre of Orpheus; and all that in Florence."[3]

I The Medici Inheritance

Florence was ruled by Lorenzo's grandfather, Cosimo de'Medici (1389–1464), who had risen from the native merchant class to a position of unprecedented influence in the affairs of his city, governing it for thirty years until his death. It is with some justice that Cosimo, and after him his son Piero and finally Lorenzo are sometimes referred to as uncrowned royalty. In fact, however, their government was nearly unique, in that

13

its effectiveness and continuity were dependent upon personal influence rather than upon institutions.[4] Cosimo was so effective in projecting the identification of his role with the interests of the city itself that after his death, he was officially accorded the title, "pater patriae."

A man of political and financial genius, Cosimo was also a key figure in maintaining Florence's primacy in the revival of learning. Keenly interested in both literature and philosophy, he collected books and established libraries, and installed first Leonardo Bruni (d. 1444), then Poggio Bracciolini (d. 1459), both leading humanists, as chancellors of the Republic. He attracted the leading scholars of his day to Florence, and handsomely rewarded their efforts, making many of them his personal friends. Marsilio Ficino (d. 1499), who under Cosimo's patronage devoted himself to philosophy, founding the Florentine Platonic Academy and translating the known works of Plato, called Cosimo his "intellectual father," and other men of Ficino's stature visited the house in the Via Larga, ate at Cosimo's table, and discussed with him their ideas.[5] It was into this atmosphere of intellectual discovery and confidence that Lorenzo was born.

The young Medici's first and most effective school was his family. His father Piero (1416–1469), although crippled with hereditary gout, continued Cosimo's patronage of letters and learning and maintained the Medici primacy in Florence until his early death. Piero's wife Lucrezia (d. 1482) was a stronger personality, and in the poetic expression of her son's later interests her influence is frequently apparent. In addition to an astuteness in political matters highly regarded even by Cosimo, Lucrezia possessed a modest literary talent and a keen interest in literary affairs. She offered continued support to several prominent writers, and wrote religious poems of a type later attempted also by Lorenzo.[6]

The earliest mentions of Lorenzo in public life serve as a revealing introduction to the man. At the festivities celebrating the visit of Pope Pius II and Galeazzo Maria Sforza, Duke of Milan, to Florence in 1459, the ten-year-old Lorenzo appeared prominently in the pageantry, and at the banquet that followed he attracted the attention of the disinguished company with a Platonic discourse on the nature of love. At the age of sixteen, he represented the Medici at the marriage of Ippolita Sforza, daughter of the ruling family of Milan, to Alfonso of Aragon— a union crucial to Medici diplomacy. Soon after, he was sent to Rome on a delicate mission in which his success exceeded expectations. In 1467, his quick-wittedness saved the life of his father, threatened by a conspiracy. Early in 1469, he appeared in a tourney held in honor of the lady of his affection, Lucrezia Donati, and his youthful exuberance carried away the prize amid public acclamation. In June of the same year he married Clarice Orsini, daughter of a noble Roman family whose alliance with the Medici was considered highly important. In December, his father Piero died; two days later, standing on the balcony of the Medici palace, he received a delegation of the leading citizens and at their request accepted the charge of the affairs of state.

II *Youthful Ruler of Florence*

When he assumed the responsibilities of government at the end of his twentieth year, Lorenzo had already demonstrated his ability to represent Florence in her relations with other cities and to control the allegiance of the Florentine people. A natural politician, he was to possess this ability to a remarkable degree to the end of his life, maintaining not only Florence's position of eminence but also his own through a period when the affairs of all the Italian states were frequently precarious. He was able to turn even the most severe reversals to his own advantage. The Pazzi conspiracy of 1478, in which his brother Giuliano was killed and he himself wounded, unified the people in his support. When the city's war with Naples led to Lorenzo's excommunication by the Pope and a papal interdiction for all of Florence, the Florentines refused to renounce their leader, and a council of Tuscan cardinals pronounced in turn against the Pope. When defeat in that war seemed imminent, Lorenzo undertook a daring personal visit to his enemy, King Alfonso of Naples, and persuaded him to reconsider his alliances and end the fighting. His diplomacy, while frequently complex, consistently bore the stamp of his own forceful personality.

During the same early years of political education that pre-

pared his entry into public life, Lorenzo also received a training
of a different kind.[7] It is an indication of the importance his
father and grandfather attached to the cause of letters and
learning that despite the early foundation of family power in
the activities of the Medici bank, Lorenzo learned little of
banking or commerce. His education was solid, classical, and
essentially literary. By all evidence he was precocious in his
studies, and his natural ability was encouraged by several of
the outstanding teachers of his day. The letters of Gentile Becchi
(d. 1496), the future Bishop of Arezzo who was his early preceptor, furnish indications of his scholarly progress in Latin.
Cristoforo Landino (d. 1498), noted for his interpretations of
the great early Italian poets as well as of the masters of the
Platonic tradition, was Lorenzo's master in poetics and rhetoric,
and beginning in 1461 he studied with Argyropoulos (d. 1487),
the Greek scholar who brought the serious study of the Greek
classics to Florence. Ficino taught him philosophy, particularly
the Renaissance strain of Platonism then evolving, which was
more an orientation of taste and a way of viewing life and
reality than a body of specific doctrines. Lorenzo himself sometimes took an active part in the meetings of the so-called Platonic
Academy founded under Ficino's influence in Florence, and his
later writings demonstrate the careful attention with which
this instruction was received.

Yet Lorenzo's youthful experience was not limited to scholarly
pursuits. In accordance with the best educational thinking of
his time, physical development was also stressed, and he excelled in many types of athletic activity, particularly in horse-
manship. His leisure hours were often spent in the countryside
or in the streets of Florence with his *brigata,* a group of young
friends, in search of amusement. Their amusement often involved
members of the opposite sex, and both Francesco Guicciardini
(d. 1540) and Niccolò Machiavelli (d. 1527) later reproached
him for his sensuality, a charge which has been alternatively
levelled and disputed by later scholars.[8] In any case, for the
varied delights and amusements offered by both city and country,
the young Medici developed an appreciation based on personal
experience that was to be a recurrent theme in his later literary work.

When, at the age of twenty, Lorenzo became the head of the Florentine state, he already had given evidence of the many-faceted personality that was to lead students of the Renaissance to consider him an enigma. Of the crucial moment when he assumed the charge of the city's affairs following his father's death, he wrote in his *Recollections*: "The second day after, when I, Lorenzo, was very young, to wit twenty-one years of age, there came to our house the principal men of the City, and of the State, to express their grief at what had happened and to comfort me. They requested that I undertake the care of the City and the State as my father and grandfather had done. To this I unwillingly assented, as not being in accord with my age, and a matter of much care and danger." While this statement, that he accepted power with some reluctance, has been ridiculed by his critics, there is no real reason to doubt its sincerity. As Horsburgh points out, the young Medici in fact had little choice: "His wealth, influence, and reputation at home and abroad, forbade him to be a private citizen. But if he was to be a public man, he must be first or nowhere."[9] He had been prepared from childhood to assume the task of wielding political power, and he wielded it with zest and consummate skill; yet he had also come to appreciate, on the one hand, his independence as a private citizen, and on the other, those activities of writing, study, and contemplation which leisure affords. He cannot have been unaware that at the age of twenty he was committing himself to a life that would demand the sacrifice of much of his privacy and most of his leisure, and whatever the political advantage, a nature as varied and as vigorous as Lorenzo's cannot have found this entirely easy to accept.

III   *The Ruler As Patron*

It is an indication of Lorenzo's attachment to his numerous other interests that he did not abandon them upon assuming the responsibilities of political power. It has been pointed out that in studying the list of his intimates "we find representatives of almost every branch of the intellectual life, but practically nobody connected with government or politics."[10] His poetry, the subject of this volume, is included in almost all anthologies of the major Italian writers, and some consider his poetic achievement among the best of his age. He was talented musically, as well, playing several instruments, and often composing songs for his group of friends. In architecture, too, he was more than an interested observer. He regretted publicly that in his period progress in architecture was not equal to that in the other arts, and after a close study of the Roman Vitruvius, he complained that the classical precepts were no longer observed. He eagerly read the treatise on architecture by L. B. Alberti (d. 1472) when it was first printed in 1485, and Poliziano, in writing the preface for that work, declared that he was following the late Alberti's plan in dedicating it to Lorenzo. Machiavelli praised his successful efforts to make his own city more beautiful through the construction of new streets and buildings; King Ferdinand of Naples consulted him about the construction of a proposed royal palace, and recent research indicates that Lorenzo himself originated plans for several outstanding architectural projects.[11]

His patronage alone, which has been the subject of numerous studies, would earn him a place of honor in the history of Italian art and letters. He freely contributed both his wealth and his influence, and the list of those who received his patronage includes the masters of the Renaissance in Florence. Among the poets and humanists were Luigi Pulci, Matteo Franco, Angelo Poliziano, Pico della Mirandola, Cristoforo Landino, Bernardo Bembo, and Marsilio Ficino; music was represented brilliantly by Antonio Squarcialupi, Arrigo Isaac, and Leonardo da Vinci. Painters such as Botticelli, Ghirlandaio, Filippino Lippi, Pollaiuolo, Verrocchio, and Da Maiano worked on his commissions and reproduced in their pictures many Medici scenes and faces. Lorenzo's collection of ancient sculpture, set up in the garden of the convent of San Marco, became a school where the young Michelangelo received his early lessons; Vasari called it a "training ground for men of genius."[12] In architecture he patronized especially Giuliano di San Gallo, who built for him the famous villa at Poggio a Caiano. He was interested, too, in the decorative arts, particularly metalwork and manuscript illumination, and few aspects of the thriving cultural life of the city escaped his attention.

Lorenzo's manuscript collection played an important part in

many of the scholarly advances of his day. Fired by the humanists' enthusiasm for classical texts, he commissioned the famous Byzantine scholar Jean Lascaris (d. 1535) to procure for him all the manuscripts he could find, obtaining some two hundred manuscripts of which Lascaris said eighty were unknown at the time. Lorenzo also sent Poliziano, the poet and humanist (d. 1494), to Ferrara, Padua, and Venice in search of codices, and others among his familiars were always alert for new acquisitions for the Medici library. Much of Lorenzo's private correspondence deals with this interest, and his collection, one of the most important of his age, was at the disposition of his humanist friends. Attempting to correct the distortions and exaggerations of the claims made later for Lorenzo's patronage, Rochon concluded that although Lorenzo was not precisely at the center of the intellectual life of his time, he nonetheless succeeded in giving to its culture a course that corresponded to his own tastes and interests.[13]

IV   *A Controversial Legacy*

Few historical figures have left behind them such a legacy of hatred and affection, scorn and admiration as that apparent in the polemic with which Lorenzo's achievement has been attacked and defended. From his own time to the present, few aspects of his life have escaped controversy. The most obvious focus of attack during his own lifetime was his conduct of the affairs of state, and the accusation of tyranny levelled by his political opponents was taken up eagerly by later critics. Although he undoubtedly ruled Florence by the exercise of exceptional personal power, the label of tyrant does not accurately describe his role in the city's affairs; in the narrow Aristotelian sense of the rule of one man in his own interests, the label is particularly inappropriate.[14] Shortly after Lorenzo's death, the Florentine government overwhelmingly voted a resolution in his praise which begins, "He always subordinated his personal interest to the good of the community," and even the anti-Medici elements of his own day conceded the advantages of his rule, as reflected in Guicciardini's famous judgment that Florence could not have had a "better and more agreeable tyrant."[15]

Modern historians point out the innovative nature of Lorenzo's conduct of the city's external affairs, particularly his conception of a league of Italian states to assure peace through a balance of power.[16] A contemporary historian called Lorenzo the "needle of the balance between the states of Italy," and the events that followed his death seemed to bear out this judgment: in 1494 the French king, Charles VIII, invaded Italy and divisions began that lasted until reunification in the nineteenth century. In the first pages of his *History of Florence,* Benedetto Varchi (d. 1565) asserted that with the death of Lorenzo one became clearly aware that "the peace and the calm of Italy, or rather of the entire world," had depended on a single man.[17]

If Lorenzo's activity had been limited to the sphere of government, the debate over his methods and motives would still make an assessment of the man difficult. Because his involvement and his influence extended also to most areas of the cultural and intellectual life of the city, and his name was linked, either as author or as patron, with many of its major achievements, the controversy about him has been particularly acute. Some have suggested merely that his nonpolitical activity could not have played a major role in a life filled with the responsibilities of government, but others have gone further, to suspect political motivation in all of his involvement in the artistic, literary, and philosophical circles of his time. His critics have deprecated his patronage by insisting that it was far from disinterested, intended either to keep the influential philosophers and writers from involving themselves in the affairs of state, or to enhance his own reputation.[18] It would be naïve to suppose that Lorenzo was unaware of the prestige he gained from his patronage and his association with the celebrated humanist and artistic circles of his day, but to assert that this convenient effect was the motivation for his involvement is too simple. The genuine appreciation of letters and the arts on which Medici patronage was consistently founded is convincingly demonstrated by the fact that it was so wisely bestowed.[19] The claim of political self-interest also fails to recognize the more important evidence, both in his own literary work and in his private correspondence, of Lorenzo's continuing personal involvement. Similarly, there are numerous indications in Lorenzo's writings that his support of Ficino and the Platonic Academy was founded in personal conviction. P. O. Kristeller has pointed out that the philosophy elaborated by Ficino, a philosophy eagerly discussed by a wide circle whose meetings frequently included Lorenzo, met a deep need of the time: "as a metaphysics based on reason and the Platonic tradition, [it] was able to satisfy the spiritual needs of those who were accustomed and inclined to hold on to Christianity and to the study of the ancients at the same time, and who were looking for a new historical and philosophical justification of their twofold commitment."[20] While it is obvious that Lorenzo could not have devoted a major portion of his time to philosophical speculation, it is difficult to deny the evidence in his own work of a serious preoccupation with several of the problems to which Ficino proposed solutions.

It was Machiavelli who, reacting to Lorenzo's versatility, phrased the impression that set the pattern for later biographers, calling him "two men joined as if by miracle."[21] The expression is itself a tribute to Lorenzo's competence in several areas, by which he seems to exemplify the Renaissance ideal. Yet Leonardo da Vinci (d. 1519) and Leon Battista Alberti, often cited as embodiments of that ideal, do not, despite their multiple talents and achievements, cause the combination of fascination and bewilderment with which many students of the Renaissance respond to Lorenzo. The reason for this difference lies perhaps in the nature of Lorenzo's activities. While Leonardo and Alberti each excelled in several areas, their multiplicity remains generally within the realm of the intelligence and the imagination; Lorenzo, on the other hand, presents that rare combination of qualities, a genius for practical affairs coupled with a significant literary talent. The treatment accorded Lorenzo by most later historians and critics clearly reveals their perplexity at the range of his interest and activity. A few openly declare their puzzlement, such as Selwyn Brinton, who demands dramatically, "Where—may I ask—and how shall we ever really grasp this Proteus of art and life? All the time the real man seems to escape us, to puzzle the historian, to elude the critic."[22] The tendency of critics, however, has been to declare one or another of his varied interests and activities to be dominant, and to reduce the others to secondary status.

V   *The Man of Letters*

Since Lorenzo was so clearly a political figure, concerned with his position as head of state and with the maintenance of Medici power, it is the man of letters who has most often been relegated to second place. Compared to his famed activity as statesman, his role as writer has received relatively little attention. His interest in literature, however, which antedated his assumption of public responsibility and continued until his death, resulted in an extensive and varied collection of works. In literary merit they range from the insignificant to an achievement equal to the best of his day, but what has been most consistently noted is their variety. In contrast to most of the major writers of his time, whose works are characterized relatively easily and who show a clear direction in the expression of their literary talents, Lorenzo attempted a wide variety of literary forms, including not only the many types of poetry that make up most of his literary production, but also the genres of drama and short story. In addition, his works vary in the extreme with regard to their inspiration: from the burlesque and the openly sensual to the Platonic and spiritual, Lorenzo's work presents an entire scale of forms and tones.

Against the background of this continuing debate, it is not surprising that Lorenzo's literary work, too, has occasioned its share of controversy. The simplest and most direct expression of criticism is again in the assertion of political motives. He has been accused of producing his works of greatest popular appeal, particularly the carnival songs, merely to divert the populace and to keep it unaware of the nature of his political activity. Girolamo Savonarola (d. 1498), the religious reformer who preached an end to the worldly splendor of Florence in the late fifteenth century, was among the first and most vehement to voice the charge that "many times the tyrant occupies the people with spectacles and celebrations so that it will think of itself and not of him," and this judgment has been repeated with minor variations through centuries of criticism of Lorenzo's poetry; Villari asserts that Lorenzo's real character appears most clearly in the dance and carnival songs as "the keen politician who wished to stupefy his people with the gross sensuality to which he himself gave way."[23] De Sanctis labelled him a "corrupt corruptor," while to Ravelli "he knew how with every means to encourage his period in all its worst tendencies: from corrupt, which it was, he made it corrupt in the extreme."[24]

The accusations that Lorenzo's poetic effort was directed toward manipulating public attitudes are easily countered. On the simplest level, such motivation could hardly account for the extent of his literary production; in addition, many works were clearly not intended for a general public, but were composed for an elite who could understand their mythological and personal allusions. Other and more serious arguments, however, have also been advanced that tend to minimize the significance of his poetry, generally based on an attempt to reconcile the activities of the poet with the demands of civil government. As his involvement in literary activity could only have been secondary in terms of time, it could not, according to this line of reasoning, have been serious, with the result that the poetry is reduced to "a form of relaxation hardly noticed in his brilliant political career."[25] Fusco dismissed as superficial most of Lorenzo's involvement with the cultural life of his time: "Those cultural splendors, those Neoplatonic discourses, that proclaimed aspiration to pure Beauty, and the stilnovistic sighing and the yearning for the solitary life, were mere tinsel, a cloak, not an inner necessity."[26] Similarly, the variety of his literary works has in itself encouraged other critics to consider Lorenzo a dilettante, whose involvement in poetry and philosophy afforded a needed and occasionally productive diversion. He has been accused of lacking poetic sincerity because of "his tendency to pass from one inspiration to another, and of his inability to fix his attention on a single subject."[27] He has been described as seeking new literary experiences each time he becomes "weary of his intellectual game."[28]

Some critics, however, have come to Lorenzo's defense. The wide range of his literary production has been accounted for in a more positive sense, as a meaningful reflection of the complexity of his own personality, or as his response to the multiple poetic traditions to which he is heir.[29] The formula of dilettantism might be partially accepted, it has been suggested, only if, "freeing it from negative connotations, one makes room for that seriousness inherent in the game, which is attested in Lorenzo's case by the rigor of his literary discipline."[30] Similarly, if dilettantism may be defined as the poet's assertion of his freedom to express the various aspects of his personality in whatever form he considers most appropriate, it is to be identified "with the very sincerity and spontaneity which are indispensable to poetry."[31]

As research into Renaissance Florence reveals more about Lorenzo and the intellectual life of which he was a part, his commitment to poetry becomes increasingly apparent. There is reason to believe that the "duality" so often noted in Lorenzo is more apparent than real, being inherent, not in the man, as Machiavelli would have it, but in his multiple frame of action. Recent criticism suggests that in the poetry, too, there is less substantial variety than previously asserted. Although his works differ in many respects, "in the great variety of Lorenzo's poetry . . . certain characteristics, the essential ones, those which make him a poet, remain constant."[32] Lorenzo himself tells us that for him the writing of poetry is a sort of *refrigerio*. This word, denoting "relaxation," also expresses "comfort" and "relief," and in this range of meaning there is an indication of the function of poetry in his life and of its frequent misinterpretation. Far from indicting his literary efforts as casual or careless, it suggests rather that poetry was the activity that, although not primary if measured in terms of time alone, nonetheless answered the deepest needs of the man, and was their most intimate expression.

CHAPTER 2

Lorenzo and the Vernacular

> *E forse saranno ancora scritte in questa
> lingua cose sottile ed importanti e degne
> d'essere lette.*[1]

LORENZO, a Tuscan like Dante, Petrarch, and Boccaccio,
was born in the century immediately following these "three
crowns" of Italian literature, whose work had seemingly assured
the triumph of the vernacular as a literary language. Within the
brief period between their lives and his, however, the literary
ascendancy of the vernacular had been seriously challenged,
with the great tradition of the fourteenth century neglected in
favor of composition in Latin. Not even these three great cham-
pions of the vernacular had used it exclusively. Dante wrote
frequently in Latin, and in that language composed the treatise
on *De vulgari eloquentia*, in which he defended the vernacular;
Petrarch expected his fame to rest on his Latin epic *Africa* and
not on his vernacular poems; and Boccaccio, heir to the scholarly
interest of Petrarch and author of several Latin works, was a
key figure in the encouragement of Greek studies in Italy. As
Kristeller reminds us, from the beginning the Italian literary
language "had to conquer its territory from medieval Latin,"
and as the Revival of Learning progressed, literary achievement
in Latin in imitation of the classical writers became the badge
of distinction.[2]

I The "Language Question"

It is important to retain a sense of balance in discussing the
"Language Question," one of the most complex in Italian literary history. Modern scholarship has increasingly suggested

25

that earlier assessments of the problem as one of hostility between Humanism and the proponents of the vernacular were at
best oversimplifications. The vernacular continued to establish
itself as an indispensable means of communication in many
areas other than literature, and even in the literary field Kristeller demonstrates that "the fifteenth century, including its
earlier phases, shows no interruption or decline in the development of vernacular prose literature, but rather an advance and
expansion, and the humanists took an active part in this
literature."[3]

It is true, however, that vernacular literary works of acknowledged merit were not being produced in the first decades of the
century. Historians of Italian literature find it difficult to
select a representative author for these years, while Croce refers
to the period 1375–1475 as "the century without poetry."[4] In
the period itself the feeling of men concerned with literature
was clearly that the vernacular was in a period of decline. The
Humanist disparagement of the great vernacular writers has no
doubt been exaggerated; yet in the historic and literary circumstances of the period, with its enthusiasm for Latin and Greek,
there were few who even attempted to equal the achievement
of Dante, Petrarch, and Boccaccio. Even in nonliterary compositions, a writer might anticipate criticism if he cast his ideas
in the vernacular. Leon Battista Alberti, for example, in composing the *Della famiglia*, expressed his awareness of this
problem, as Lorenzo was to do years later in beginning his own
Comento, and justified his choice by his desire to be understood by all instead of by a privileged few. Similarly, in the
prelude to his *Teogenio*, Alberti records that "many blame me,
and say that I offend literary grandeur, not writing on such an
eloquent subject in the Latin language."[5]

By the end of the fifteenth century, the language question
was again resolved in favor of the vernacular, whose primacy
in literary expression was now assured, and the period when
this battle was won coincides in large part with Lorenzo's life.
The lasting importance of the Medici contribution during this
critical phase of the linguistic crisis is generally acknowledged,
and took three major forms—in theory, in practice, and in
patronage.

II   *Lorenzo's Choice of the Vernacular*

All of Lorenzo's own literary works are composed in the vernacular. He did not choose the *volgare* because he found the use of Latin difficult or awkward; as a schoolboy he tried his hand at Latin poetry before attempting verse in Italian, and from his youth occasionally used Latin in correspondence, notably with Ficino.[6] His letter to the Pope in response to the excommunication of Florence is considered a fine and impassioned example of Latin prose. It has been suggested that his choice was due to the limited time he was able to devote to his literary work, but Lorenzo was not a casual poet, and his choice of the vernacular cannot plausibly be seen as mere preference for an easy medium. On the contrary, his choice may appear somewhat surprising, since his grandfather and father had taken the lead in encouraging Humanist scholarship and the collection and copying of classical texts. It is, in fact, an argument against the accusation of dilettantism that Lorenzo did not choose to exercise his literary talent in the medium most in favor at the moment; it may be argued that, given his education and his demonstrated responsiveness to the intellectual trends of his time, the writing of Latin verse would have been more facile—and certainly more prestigious—than the exercise of his ability in the vernacular. Whatever the reason for his preference, it is certain that the result of his choosing the vernacular for his own works was to enhance its prestige as a literary language.

Developments in the Florence of Lorenzo's time and aspects of his own education reveal that his choice had been well prepared. In 1436, Leonardo Bruni, one of the ablest and most influential of the "first-generation" Humanists in Florence, published his *Vite di Dante e di Petrarca*, which, in Baron's opinion, "initiated the active interest of the Florentine humanists in the Volgare."[7] Even before, Giovanni da Prato, in writing his *Paradiso degli Alberti*, had felt "the ardent desire, which spurs me on incessantly, to exalt our mother-tongue as well as I can and know, and to ennoble it in the way it has already been ennobled and exalted by the three crowns of Florence more than by anybody else."[8] Influenced by Bruni and the linguistic controversies of the period, Alberti wrote of the great potential of the vernacular, which would be recognized "if only our learned men will make every effort to refine and polish it by their studies and labors."[9] Cristoforo Landino, too, one of the most noted Humanist grammarians and a poet in his own right, appreciated the poetic heritage of the vernacular, freely imitating both Dante and Boccaccio in his Latin *Xandra*. Called to lecture on poetics at the Studio of Florence, he devoted a year to Petrarch, opening the series of lectures with an important oration defending the study of a vernacular author.[10] In a later commentary to Dante's *Divine Comedy* he laid the foundation for a reconciliation between the claims of Latin and those of the vernacular, with the assertion that the study of Latin is the only means of achieving excellence in the *volgare*. Taking Dante as the example and later writers as illustration, he explained, as Baron points out, that "there is, therefore, no conflict between the Latin and the vernacular studies; the humanistic cultivation of Latin is needed in the very interest of the Volgare."[11]

In Lorenzo's case, the personal preference for the vernacular was prepared from early childhood. In the house of his grandfather Cosimo he was on familiar terms with men who knew and appreciated the vernacular masterpieces. His first preceptor, Gentile Becchi, communicated his love for Dante while providing a solid classical education. Probably even more influential in the formation of the young Medici's taste were three other intimates of the Medici household: Landino, whose courses at the Studio Lorenzo probably followed from 1458; Marsilio Ficino; and Luigi Pulci.[12] Pulci especially, although older than Lorenzo by seventeen years, was frequently a genial participant in the prince's youthful *brigata*, and his letters provide much of our information about its activities. His own preferences helped to determine the literary direction of the group, and in a time when such scholar-writers as Ficino, Landino, and later Poliziano held center-stage, Pulci proclaimed that his own muse was of the domestic variety.[13]

The concern with the medium of literary expression, which Lorenzo early acquired and which was of the greatest importance in his formation as writer, thus came from the two strong influences in his development—the realist strain and the classicist-philosophical. De Robertis suggests that the two aspects or poles so often noted in Lorenzo's work "correspond to easily recognizable faces. Pulci and Ficino are the protagonists (and the antagonists) of Lorenzo's literary initiation."[14] And the literary attitudes of these men, so different in other respects, combined to develop in Lorenzo an interest in the expressive potential of the vernacular and a concern for its development that was both practical and philosophical.

Against this background, it is not surprising that all of Lorenzo's literary works are cast in the vernacular. The attitudes determining this choice need not be merely inferred from his practice, however, as there are among his writings both a defense of the *volgare* and an appreciation of its importance. These are found principally in two works: in the famous *Epistola* or letter to Frederic of Aragon, which accompanied the so-called *Raccolta Aragonese*, a collection of early Tuscan poems, and in the *Comento* or commentary which Lorenzo composed for a number of his own sonnets. Although the authorship of the *Epistola* is disputed, there is general agreement that the *Raccolta* itself, in its selection of poems, reflects Lorenzo's poetic preference, and that the letter reflects at least his general ideas. Even if not by his own hand, they have a place in any consideration of Lorenzo's work for their important evidence of his literary attitudes, especially since this evidence is supported by the treatment of the vernacular found in the *Comento*.

III *The* Epistola *to Frederic of Aragon*

The *Raccolta Aragonese*, often considered the first anthology of Italian poetry, was sent by Lorenzo to Frederic of Aragon, son of the king of Naples, probably in 1476.[15] The exact contents of the original *Raccolta* are uncertain, but it contained a heavy concentration of *dolce stil nuovo* poems, and perhaps both Dante's *Vita Nuova* and Boccaccio's *Vita di Dante*, concluding with some poems by Lorenzo himself.[16] Its accompanying letter explains that this collection of Tuscan poems was put together to comply with a specific request by Frederic. More than a simple letter introducing the collection to its distinguished addressee, the *Epistola*, which presents a brief history of vernacular poetry in Italy and an assessment of its development, merits the description of "first document, after the *De vulgari eloquentia*, of a critical history of Italian poetry."[17] As a theoretical work, it demonstrates that the choice and grouping of the poems in the *Raccolta* correspond to well-defined criteria.[18]

The *Epistola* opens with a discussion of "ancient times," and almost half of it develops the theme of the relationship between "illustrious and virtuous works" and poetry in general.[19] In the introductory section, the author maintains that one of the principal merits of the glorious past age was that every great work was accorded great reward and praise, both public and private; the greatness of the achievement of that age, he continues, may be attributed to this one fact, since honor nourishes every art, and the promise of glory incites mortals to greatness. For this reason, the Greeks and Romans naturally valued those who could render great deeds immortal through the power of poetry. It was Homer who assured the fame of Achilles; for without this "divine poet," a single tomb would have buried the fame of the hero along with his body.

This valuation of the poet as one who assures the fame of greatness, and the valuation of poetry as that which in its turn, by promising the immortality of fame, inspires to greatness, has a familiar ring; Petrarch had stressed it a century earlier, and the derivations from Petrarch's works are varied and striking throughout the letter.[20] But here the praise of hero and poet acquires an additional element. If the fame of Achilles would not have survived without a Homer, it is also true that the poems of Homer would not themselves have survived without the aid of an enlightened prince, Pisistratus of Athens, who had the poet's works collected and preserved, and thus acquired immortal glory also for himself.

The author of the *Epistola* links ancient times to his own, effecting a transition to his discussion of the state of vernacular letters. After the great period of antiquity there followed one in which rewards for great deeds were lacking. Greatness was lacking too, and this in turn caused the poets to be neglected. For this reason many of the great classical authors are lost to us. But even in the midst of this cultural decline, the author asserts, there were poets who began to cultivate the neglected Italian language with such skill that it is now in full flower. Here the analogy carefully prepared in the introductory section is completed: as the Athenian prince honored Homer, so the Renaissance prince honors his own outstanding poets. Some critics have seen this praise of the patron in the *Epistola* as an indication of Poliziano's authorship.[21] The question of patronage was, of course, one of major importance to Poliziano; to emphasize this aspect, however, is to ignore the stress of the presentation in the letter. The author does not praise Pisistratus merely as a defender of letters; the prince is praised because the defense of letters is useful. The final exclamation of the section, which includes in its reference the hero, the poet, and now the ruler, is "O truly divine men, and born into the world for the good of mankind!" and this emphasis accords too well with Lorenzo's own interests, particularly with his own conception of the role of ruler-patron, to be easily dismissed. His thinking was profoundly influenced by central figures in the movement of vernacular humanism, particularly by Landino and Alberti, and the stress on the civic function of language—an integral part of vernacular humanism—has important implications for the evaluation of Lorenzo's involvement in the literary life of his time.

In fact, the author of the *Epistola* may well have had in mind the specific efforts to connect the vernacular with civic virtue which were already associated with the Medici name. Among the praiseworthy customs of the past, for example, he notes particularly "the contest of poetry and oratory." In 1441, a few years before Lorenzo's birth, Alberti had obtained the support and financial backing of Piero de'Medici in an attempt to transplant the classical *certame coronario*, a poetic competition, to Florentine soil. This effort, although abortive, was effective in focusing attention on the vernacular and its claims; and Alberti's promotion of the competition, like the defense of poetry in the letter, was in terms of the widest civic benefit.[22] We may also suspect in the letter's lament for lost manuscripts an indirect reference to the efforts made under Cosimo's sponsorship to collect, edit, and preserve major classical texts. Although the Medici name is never mentioned in the *Epistola,* by 1476 these efforts were receiving wide acclaim throughout Italy and abroad.

The letter tells us that men during the postclassical period allowed the loss of so many great classical authors because they were themselves lacking in virtue and merit, and thus could not appreciate the great writers who celebrated great deeds. The implication is clear, especially as the letter was written to accompany and recommend a collection of poetry, that with the advent of Medici rule this period of cultural decline was drawing to an end. Hints of a new age of great deeds and great poetry, a new "Golden Age," appear repeatedly in Florentine art and literature during the period of Lorenzo's youth, as does the suggestion that Lorenzo, "Lauro," in his multiple role of prince-poet-patron, is at its center.[23]

The second section of the *Epistola* deals specifically with the vernacular. Defending the potential of the vernacular for poetic use, the author claims that if it be well and justly evaluated, it will be found to be neither poor nor rough. He illustrates his contention through a brief critical assessment of early poetry, with special praise for Dante, Petrarch, and Cavalcanti, the emphasis on Cavalcanti reflecting Ficino's Neoplatonic interpretation of that poet.[24] Although such a critical effort applied to the vernacular is itself new, it is particularly noteworthy for its appreciation of one aspect of the vernacular poetic tradition, that of the *dolce stil nuovo* or "sweet new style." This emphasis stands in proportion to the actual composition of the collection, where stilnovistic poems predominate, and provides a valuable clue to Lorenzo's own poetic evolution. Although the chronology of his poems is generally uncertain, it is possible to distinguish in them two principal styles. Lorenzo seems to have been the first of his circle to incorporate obvious stilnovistic elements into his work, and the chronological distinction between the earlier (Petrarcan) and later (stilnovistic) styles has been posited as 1476–77, partly on the evidence that none of the poems by Lorenzo included in the *Raccolta* are in the later manner.[25]

IV *The* Comento

This consideration of Lorenzo's poetic evolution leads to the *Comento,* his commentary to some of his sonnets, where he himself suggests that his new style was introduced after the death of Simonetta Vespucci (in 1476) and the composition of his poems in her honor.[26] The *Comento* too is difficult to date with precision, but recent work has suggested that it may have been begun during the same time the *Epistola* was composed, a coincidence in date which would lend added significance to any similarities in ideas and presentation between these two works. There are in fact a number of striking correspondences which link the *Comento* and the letter. Both are written as commentaries about poems, and both concern themselves in part with poetry in general, defending its importance with both social and esthetic arguments. Especially significant in both works is the support of the claims of poetry in the vernacular.

Noting in the *Comento* that some find the vernacular "not capable or worthy of any excellent matter or subject,"[27] Lorenzo sets out criteria by which a language may be evaluated. He notes that the first two of these—copiousness and abundance, and ability to express well any concept of the mind—are inherent in the language itself, while the others—sweetness and harmoniousness relative to other languages, and the evidence of great works written in it—are more subjective. He then calls upon experience as the best measure, pointing out that Dante, Petrarch and Boccaccio had shown that any meaning can be expressed with sweetness and harmony in the vernacular. While this justification in general follows the defense of the vernacular in Dante's *Convivio,* the degree of imitation has often been exaggerated. Lipari's comments are more fair to Lorenzo, noting that the poet's opinion is "the result of study, and frequently involved the introduction of new points in favor of Italian," with the result that "Lorenzo does not precisely copy his Italian model. He knows it, adapts it to his case, and—as it were—brings the *Convivio* up to date."[28]

Lorenzo's lead in assuming the defense of the vernacular in the *Comento* is widely recognized, along with the fact that his arguments bear many similarities, both in type and in detail, to those found in the *Epistola.* Critics who have compared the two works in the hope of resolving the question of the letter's authorship have generally stressed their differences rather than their similarities, particularly the confrontation of the vernacular with Latin in the *Comento*; but these differences may also be ascribed to the different contexts in which the discussion occurs.[29] The author of the *Epistola*, introducing a wide-ranging anthology of vernacular poetry, attempts to demonstrate by these examples that good poetry could be, and had been, written in the vernacular; as the *Raccolta* was presumably sent in response to Frederic's request for such a compilation, no detailed defense need be offered for the vernacular as such. In the *Comento*, on the other hand, Lorenzo presents his comments on the vernacular as a response to anticipated criticism for having used it for his own poetry; he thus focuses on establishing the worthiness of his chosen literary language, and in doing so must directly counter the main thrust of that criticism, that Latin would have been more suitable on several counts.

On the positive side, it appears that the attitudes that seem most original in the *Epistola* are particularly meaningful with respect to Lorenzo's unique position as poet, patron, and head-of-state. The glorification of the role of ruler-patron, adduced in support of Poliziano's authorship, and the stress on usefulness as a justification for the vernacular, are consistent with Lorenzo's own conception of his role. The added dimension of states-manship makes the suggested relationship between Tuscan and classical history in the *Epistola* particularly noteworthy. This, too, finds a parallel in the *Comento*, with the idea that the future perfection of the still-adolescent vernacular will be joined to the success and expansion of Florence herself.[30]

Lorenzo's authorship of the *Epistola* thus appears plausible enough on several counts to leave the question of attribution open.[31] But whatever its solution, two significant points emerge from the letter and the defense of the vernacular in the *Comento*. First, Lorenzo's use of the vernacular rather than Latin for his own literary works reflects a deliberate choice related to a conception of the "Language Question" within a wide civic context. Second, these works demonstrate that he knew the Italian poetic tradition as perhaps few others of his day, and that he drew conclusions about it with independence and originality. These points indicate both that the nature of his interest and involvement in the subject of the vernacular was complex, and that his attention to poetry was far from superficial.

CHAPTER 3

Life Observed and Transformed

THREE poems, the *Uccellagione*, the *Simposio*, and the *Nencia da Barberino*, represent the early period of Lorenzo's poetic activity. They are among his earliest literary efforts, all probably composed before or during 1474, and all suggest more or less directly the context of his youthful *brigata* or group of friends. All may be classified loosely as "realistic" in that they directly reflect the life around him: two relate episodes presented as part of his own experience—a day of hunting, an encounter with drunkards upon returning to Florence—and the third is set in Barberino, a village in the Tuscan countryside.

The three poems as a group offer a triple view of Lorenzo's world. The *Uccellagione* or falcon hunt presents the day's amusement of a small aristocratic band; the frenzied activity of the drunkards in the *Simposio* is set against a background of city crowds and movement; the enamored peasant Vallera expresses his love for Nencia of Barberino in terms that reveal his own humble context. While the focus of the three poems varies widely —from the social level of Lorenzo's own friends, to city-dwellers, to a country swain—none of the poems assumes the mythological or Platonic guise frequent in Lorenzo's later works. Each is Lorenzo's imaginative recreation—whether by implied participation, comic exaggeration, or amused but sympathetic detachment—of one small portion of that Tuscan world that formed the setting of his own youthful activities.

Lorenzo's own reaction to the life around him shapes and guides each poem. All three works are animated by the author's amused participation in the small drama he creates. In all of them, the comic note is fundamental, with comic exaggeration ranging from the petty quarrels of the *Uccellagione's* hunters

35

and the naïve praises of Nencia's admirer to the gross distortions and excesses of the *Simposio*'s drunkards. There are occasional serious notes, but the weariness and the spiritual uncertainty that characterized much of Lorenzo's poetry late in his life are absent in these poems.

While clear precedents in the earlier Italian tradition may be found for the form of each of these poems, the element of derivation is minimal. The poetic merit of the works ranges from the dubious comic effect of the *Simposio* to the rare freshness and spontaneity of the *Nencia*, frequently considered Lorenzo's masterpiece. As a group, however, they demonstrate, even at this early period of Lorenzo's literary activity, both the young poet's acute observation of his world, and his genuine skill and originality in its imaginative transformation.

I *The* Uccellagione di starne

The work of Lorenzo's that seems the most direct reflection of an episode of his own life is the *Uccellagione di starne*, a poem of forty-five octaves frequently referred to as the *Caccia col falcone*.[1] Several of the named participants are identifiable, among them such well-known personages as Luigi Pulci, and this fact has made possible the use of biographical data to produce an approximate dating for the work. The poem apparently presents a typical day of falconry by that little *brigata* or group of friends with whom Lorenzo was associated during the years 1465–1468. Its composition may date from that early period of his life, although it has also been suggested that the work describes a particular hunt that took place between 1472 and 1474.[2] It is written in the first person, with the poet himself figuring in the events narrated, and by all indications Lorenzo wrote it shortly after an actual day of hunting, primarily for the amusement of the group. The last two lines form a *congedo*, which indicates that he prepared his account as a description for an absent friend: "and thus, comrade, I happily pass the time." This *compare*, or comrade, seems himself to have been a real person, as the word appears in several documents as the nickname of one of the members of the *brigata*.[3]

A type of poetry known generally as the *caccia* had enjoyed some popularity in the preceding century, and Lorenzo, familiar with the literary heritage of his region, almost certainly had read or heard poems of this type. These works are difficult to describe, and have been characterized as "between lyric and dramatic, between madrigal and eclogue."[4] Even the meaning of the name is in doubt, perhaps deriving from the content of the poems (although only about half of them deal with hunting), or perhaps from musical terms for "canon," as they were apparently written to be sung in this form by two or three voices.[5] While they may have furnished Lorenzo with the idea of writing his poem, familiarity in this case does not indicate derivation in any significant sense, and Lorenzo produces a work which is both quite personal and different from any other poem of the type.[6] Similarly, the autobiographical element should not be too heavily stressed. The recording of a day's hunting activity for the absent friend may have been the incentive to commit the account to paper. But as it takes poetic form, this record becomes in Lorenzo's hands a work of literature, revealing a fundamental artistic impulse and a "narrative cohesion" which set it apart.[7]

Hunting was one of Lorenzo's favorite pastimes. His passion for it is attested in letters and records, such as in Poliziano's account to Lorenzo's wife Clarice of one stay in the country. Lorenzo, Poliziano reports, had found a fine falcon: "Lorenzo is so enamoured of it that it's incredible. And to tell the truth, he's not wrong; for maestro Giorgio says he has never seen a more handsome or a larger one, and he intends to make it the best falcon in the world."[8] The inclusion of much precise detail in the *Uccellagione* reveals both Lorenzo's real delight in the sport and his familiarity with all its aspects. He does not hesitate to use technical words associated with the hunt when they suit his purpose; in fact, as Rochon points out, the concrete presentation of the hunting scenes gives the poem a more immediate documentary interest than do the treatises of falconry like Frederic II's famous *De arte venandi cum avibus*.[9] One of the poem's chief merits rests on Lorenzo's ability to capture precisely the line of a gesture, the moment when an action is at its peak, and to render them direct and whole to his reader; the essential drama of each moment is conveyed.

However precise and vivid the detail of the hunt, this realistic note is not Lorenzo's focus. The manner in which the hunters are portrayed makes this clear. The poet, although a participant in the episodes related, is primarily an observer, but as observer he is neither detached nor disinterested. His tone is one of "affectionate mockery," established with the first episode which focuses on a single individual:[10] "But Fortune, which always enjoys making brown that which is most white, made Dionigi, who fell asleep, fall, and unfortunately to his left." The fall to the left is unfortunate because Dionigi thus falls on his hawk, injuring it severely. He is secretly pleased, thinking he has thus escaped further exertion. But when he attempts to bring the bird back to its post, the hawk bites him; and without further ado, Dionigi "throws it down, leaps on it, and deals it an awful blow." The characterization of Dionigi as a lazy type who much regrets having been obliged to leave his bed is continued later in the poem, for it is he, "all red, sweating like a fresh egg," who insists that the day is too hot for the sport to continue. And the comic interest is visible in the nature of the episodes themselves, where one minor crisis follows another. As Rochon points out, "Lorenzo has attributed to his friends more misadventures than they could plausibly experience in a few hours. And at the same time, he lends a humorous tone to events which could have been related in a serious manner."[11]

Yet neither the realistic nor the comic strain, both highly developed in the poem, conveys the essential conception. Lorenzo's basic interest is not in the hunt itself, but rather in the involvement of men in the hunt: the robust activity of healthy men on a perfect day, the appreciation of the activity not in itself but as a manifestation. This emphasis on the human is apparent in the large proportion of character portrayal, however caricatural and teasing it may be; the direct narration of the hunt takes second place to descriptions of nature and passages of direct discourse, so that much of the poem reads like a miniature drama. The emphasis is also reflected in the poem's structure, where the hunt is integrated at beginning and end into a more general setting. The first two stanzas present the awakening of the day, which precedes the awakening of the hunter. Both animal life and the humble peasant are included in the anticipation of the fair morning:

> All of the east was already red
> and the mountain tops looked like gold;
> the little swallow was making a great racket,
> and the peasant returned to his labor . . .
> Already the solicitous peasant woman
> had opened the door for the sheep and the pigs.
> The air was clear, fresh and crystalline,
> and the morning gave hope of good weather.

The hunters awaken to the sounds of preparation, and from that point "brisk human activity dominates in the world."[12] Symmetrically, the account of the hunt itself concludes with the return of the hunters, their eager attack on the waiting feast, their conversation and particularly their good-humored boasting of the merits of their hawks; but the poem concludes with all retiring at day's end.

It is important that the activity that forms the poem's subject is that of a group. Lorenzo attempts to portray his friends "in their most spontaneous movements and reactions,"[13] and it is to the functioning of the group as such that he particularly responds. His concern for it is reflected in the care with which he describes the positions of each major participant in the hunt, both men and dogs.[14] It also explains the importance accorded the quarrel between two of the hunters, Guglielmo and Foglia. Their hawks fight; and following the example of the birds, the men almost fight too. Guglielmo first believes that his bird has won in the fight, and being reproached, repeatedly insists that he has seen nothing; but when it becomes apparent that his is the injured bird, he becomes enraged and begins to threaten Foglia. He will be prudent, he says, but he will not forget, and warns that the two will meet again (stanza 36).

The quarrel remains unresolved while the hunters return to their lodging and begin their feast. Some critics have considered this episode weak because its potential for comedy is not fully exploited.[15] While it has its own tone of subdued comedy, however, it is not included primarily for comic effect. Its significance is that the quarrel disturbs the equilibrium of the sport and of the day, which has been one of good-natured participation and camaraderie. This is why no one forgets it, and why the group does not take it lightly: "Foglia's quarrel with Guglielmo was

spoiling everything" (stanza 43). One member assumes the role
of peacemaker, so that at the end harmony is restored with a
reconciliation; and "with this done, each one goes off to sleep"
(stanza 44).

It has been suggested that the appeal of the hunt for Lorenzo
is that of "a fine game, in which men become as noisy and
innocent as boys."[16] While this notion of the hunt as a boisterous
pursuit perhaps fails to give adequate weight to the serious
dimension of Lorenzo's attitude, it is suggestive in another
sense, not for the effects of the game on its participants, but in
the nature of game as activity. As a stylization of human relationships, it has an esthetic dimension, and this colors Lorenzo's
appreciation of the sport. It is apparent from the beginning, in
the opening passage discussed above. The description of the
new morning is full of realistic detail, closely observed; but
this everyday reality, with all its humble content, contributes
to a poetic effect where "all the particulars are fused into a
single atmosphere, which brings them together, in the constancy
of the lyric impression: freshness of the world, freshness of the
awakening."[17] Because the criterion for the selection of the
details is a poetic one, the result is the creation of "a pretty
air of fable."[18]

We see, then, that Lorenzo's unpretentious little poem is
rather complex. Despite its air of easy informality, it is not
artless. The apparent spontaneity is achieved through careful
control. The rhythms vary with the atmosphere to be created:
excitement, haste, suspense, fatigue, joking relaxation, anger,
relief—which alternate to sustain interest. Opening with the
establishment of both a setting and a tone through the awakening of human activity, the poem concludes with the return of
the hunters at the end of that activity, such that the carefully
elaborated structural equilibrium is a parallel to the human
equilibrium of group activity established during the course of
the hunt itself.[19] Neither comedy nor realism, both of which
have been suggested as the fundamental notes of the poem, are
at its core; they are manners controlled by the poet in order
to convey his amused and indulgent enjoyment of this small
human drama.

II *The* Simposio

In the *Simposio*, also called the *Beoni* or "drunkards," the author relates that, returning one autumn day to Florence along the road that leads to the Faenza Gate, he found the streets full of hurrying people. Inquiring of a friend, Bartolino, he learns that all are hurrying to the Rifredi bridge, where the innkeeper Giannese has spilled a keg of wine. Bartolino satisfies the author's curiosity about many of the people who are passing by, and a number of these are persuaded to stop and relate their own stories. A second guide, Ser Nastagio, then takes the place of Bartolino who rushes on his way. Nastagio points out more drunkards to the ever curious author until the poem breaks off, unfinished, in chapter 8.[20]

The *Simposio* furnishes an example of the variety of difficulties encountered in dealing with Lorenzo's works. There is almost no aspect on which critics have agreed: its date, its manner of composition, its tone and intent, and most recently and fundamentally, its structure have all been disputed. Like the *Uccellagione*, it mentions a number of real persons, and, as with the hunting poem, attempts to date it have proceeded by the establishment of biographical data about those who may be identified. Rochon used this method to establish a *post quem* of 1473, and opted for 1474 as the probable date of composition.[21] More recent research has radically altered that picture to a *post quem* of 1466 and an *ante quem* of late 1469, thus placing the work among the compositions of Lorenzo's youthful period, perhaps even during the years before he assumed the responsibilities of state.[22]

The fact that the work, as we know it, is incomplete, has also been the subject of controversy. Niccolo Valori relates that Lorenzo, seeing the drunkards as he returned from his villa at Careggi, began *and completed* an improvised poem on the subject, but the work is unfinished in all the manuscripts.[23] Rochon points out that despite Lorenzo's inclination to improvise he could hardly have composed some eight hundred verses during that short journey, and concludes that he must have sketched a few passages along the way, later integrating them into a longer work which he never completed.[24] Martelli, however, convinced that Valori actually knew of the existence of the completed work he mentions, advances the theory that the poem passed through various redactions: that Lorenzo completed a brief satiric poem in the days immediately following the encounter, but later took it up again as the basis for the incomplete longer poem which we know.[25] And the incomplete text itself has been the object of important criticism. In the edition of the *Simposio* he published in 1966, Martelli denied the standard presentation of the work in eight chapters and a fragment of a ninth, and his re-editing results in a more coherent structure, radically affecting our understanding of the poem.[26]

The work receives its title from its references to the gathering of drunkards. These *beoni* are such exaggerated figures that the work has been described as "the peak of mockery and of caricature," and Carducci considered it an important contribution to this type of writing.[27] The drunkards are indicated to the author by two others, who are themselves driven by the same thirst. All classes of society are represented and portrayed in such a way that many individuals can be identified even after the passage of several centuries. The unflattering nature of this presentation has led some to consider Lorenzo's poem a means of attack on his enemies, but this view is easily refuted.[28] In the first place, most of those included were not Medici enemies, the best example being the fat man who, when invited to dinner, "goes with an empty cask and returns with a full one" ("va botticello e torna botte piena"), an apparent punning allusion to the painter Sandro Botticelli, who was one of Lorenzo's favorites.[29] While several of the men presented were well known as *beoni,* some not possessed of this thirst may have been included as part of the joke; we may even assume that some would have been flattered, understanding the spirit of the work and the intent of its prestigious author.

Nonetheless, Lorenzo's attitude must be carefully assessed. As in the *Caccia,* the author appears in the *Simposio* as both narrator and personage, and again he is apparently detached. But his account is not characterized by any pretense of objectivity. The poem at its beginning invokes the aid of Bacchus, who "is seen going about through the towns and in every path" (I, 10–12). The author's attitude is also indicated at the beginning of chapter II: when the narrator first becomes acquainted with the situation of the drunkards, his reaction is "part of laughter and part of shame for that which he had seen and heard." The *beoni* are recognized as excessive in their thirst and ridiculous in their drunken conduct, but the thirst itself is not attacked; the narrator does not rebuke his guide's sympathy for the man who, having lost his thirst, declares himself ready to "renounce life" if he cannot regain it: "Now follow the road, my guide said, and may God restore your lost thirst" (VII, 123–24). The smile with which the narrator himself surveys these men is certainly not one of "Mephistophelian scorn," nor does he set out to present a picture of the fundamental baseness and depravity of mankind, as one critic has insisted.[30] His descriptions, while certainly not flattering, seem at least in most cases good-natured and teasing rather than condemning or even harsh, and the exaggeration contributes to this effect, since accuracy is clearly not intended.

While the detail of the poem has its source in Lorenzo's own acute observation and in his imaginative transformation of everyday reality, the work also has clearly identifiable literary sources. These are of two major types: the poetry of Dante and Petrarch, and the poems written at a later date to parody the imitators of these masters. Several well-known works of the period written in imitation of Dante or Petrarch consist of catalogues of various types of people; others use the pretext of a vision or a fantastic voyage, adapted from the *Commedia* or from Petrarch's *Trionfi*, to present the allegorical adventures of their author and his guides. Most of these works have very little literary merit, and the types were abused to the extent that they soon became the subject of parody by Burchiello and other popularizers who were widely read and appreciated during the first half of the fifteenth century.[31] Both sources, the fourteenth-century masterpieces and their parodies, are such obvious influences in the *Simposio* that De Robertis considered the true subject of Lorenzo's poem to be the vernacular tradition itself, in its most prestigious forms, but rendered in a key of parody and burlesque.[32]

Lorenzo's use of Dante's *Commedia* is obvious even to the casual reader. The author-protagonist is provided with a guide who indicates to him the most notable figures in the throng. The manner in which he addresses them, the substitution of a second guide for the first, the use of Dante's verse form, even the detail of many episodes—all are more or less transparent borrowings. In Dante's poem, the persons are usually introduced in action or by description before being identified by name; in Lorenzo's poem, the narrator says "Oh my Bartolo, who do I see sitting there,—I began,—over there near Romituzzo?—And he to me:— It's a man who wants to enjoy" (I, 64–66). In the *Commedia*, the positions of the heavenly bodies are repeatedly used for orientations in time and space; in the *Simposio*, the author indicates for example that "the sun had already risen to midday, so that it shortened all the shadows, already almost meeting the Great and the Little Bear" (VII, 1–3).

Both relationships between characters and individual details are frequently drawn from Dante's work. Virgil is introduced by Dante as one "who through long silence seemed weak," and Lorenzo gives us "one who through too much drinking was already weak." In the *Commedia*, sinners refer to the wrong-doings that brought them to perdition, while one of Lorenzo's drunkards insists "and of that which I've done, I don't repent, even in these torments" (II, 43–45). Virgil and later Beatrice anticipate the pilgrim Dante's questions, and Lorenzo's guide is similarly quick: "I lent an ear to his words; and he added that he saw that I was preparing to ask more:—I know, before it's said, your desire; and I'll make you aware of this with a proof, for I will demonstrate it through my speech" (III, 40–45). The incident in Purgatory where Dante attempts without success to embrace Casella is used twice in succession by Lorenzo: "and then wanting to embrace my guide, he veered toward him, but the wave led him elsewhere, and an embrace of his companions: just like a dog who crosses a river with great effort, and thinks he is going directly opposite, but the full current leads him further down" (VII, 31–36), followed by "three times he attempted to embrace him, three times he held out his hands in that direction, three times his hands touched his own chest" (VII, 100–102).

Some have seen this parodying of Dante and Petrarch, and particularly of the *Commedia*, as the distinctive aspect of the *Simposio*, and have judged it harshly. Carducci was particularly offended, insisting that many would be disgusted by the frequent use of Dante's techniques in such a poem.[33] But such offense at the "disrespectful" use of Dante and of Petrarch is based on a misunderstanding of Lorenzo's times and of his intentions. In the first place, Lorenzo so frequently expressed and demonstrated his admiration for these earlier poets that it is difficult to interpret his work as intended to ridicule them or to produce laughter at their expense. And even within the *Simposio*, Lorenzo's debt to the *Commedia* is not primarily in terms of parody; Dante had effectively used a variety of techniques to maintain the curiosity and interest of his reader, and Lorenzo, recognizing this achievement, uses many of them for his own, radically different purpose.[34]

Further evidence that his satiric use of his sources is not directed against them is found in the similar treatment of other authors and themes. Lorenzo's devotion to Ficino and his ideas is not open to question, nor is the fact that he himself sponsored and participated in a number of the banquets of the Florentine Academy; yet the *Simposio* contains frequent comic references to Ficino and to his works, and here, too, are found examples of direct parody. In the lines "if they are capital enemies of wine, then the wine is their capital enemy, for it directs its furor of wine to the head" (VI, 94–96) is clearly a play on words based on the title of Ficino's work *De Furore divino* of 1457. The title *Simposio* itself not only suggests Plato's work of that name, but also the taste of Ficino and the other members of the Florentine Academy for banquets, a celebrated preference that probably combined with "simposio's" early meaning of "drinking party" to suggest the title of Lorenzo's poem. And to this may be added Lorenzo's extensive and obvious parody of his own work, particularly his youthful Petrarcan poems.[35]

Like his "disrespectful" use of earlier writers, Lorenzo's use of thinly veiled biblical allusions has also aroused indignation. Horsburgh calls the reference to the thirst of Christ on the cross "perhaps the most revolting conceit in literature," and refuses even to translate the stanza, adding that mere quotation "seems an insult to the reader which demands an apology."[36] Other allusions to the life of Christ appear in the work, for

example in the well-known story of the *piovano* (rector) Arlotta
and his friend. The adventure of these men, who "rose again on
the third day" after a bout of drinking because they had "opened
a certain cupboard thinking it was a window, and seeing it
dark, hurried back to bed," to sleep until awakened, is compared
to the "divine miracle" by which Christ halted the sun (VIII,
34–48). Yet while such comparisons may offend the modern
reader, criticism such as that of Horsburgh takes these passages
much more seriously than they would have been taken by Lorenzo and his contemporaries, who would not have seen them
as blasphemy nor as any indication of irreligion. In Lorenzo's
time, such use of religious allusion, when clearly intended within
its context for comic effect alone, was neither shocking nor
uncommon.

What conclusions may be drawn, then, about this poem, which
has been Lorenzo's "most mistreated and neglected work?"[37] In
the first place, it should not be read as a product of a "freakish twist" in Lorenzo's nature, or a "psychological product"
both "curious and baffling," but rather as a literary work.[38] We
may discard the notion of straightforward moralizing on the
evil effects of wine, while admitting that a mild lesson to this
effect may emerge. So too, the notion that Lorenzo was carica-
turing his contemporaries as a form of attack ought to be
dismissed. In addition, Lorenzo had no intention of ridiculing
Dante, Petrarch, or any other figure in the Italian literary tradition, although these contribute his basic materials. Instead,
he drew freely on his own literary tradition to create a vehicle
for observations drawn from life, combining the two for comic
effect. The basic disproportion between the noble language and
gesture, appropriate to lofty poems like those of Dante and
Petrarch, and the low level of the subject and its treatment is
in fact fundamental to the comic impression.[39] The presentation
of the drunkards and the use of literary allusion are both determined by a single objective: to laugh and to cause laughter,[40]
and perhaps the most important observation to be made about
Lorenzo's laughter in this poem is that it is not directed against
anything, be it the literary tradition or the drunkards described.

The evaluation of the work as literature remains difficult. Even
with the improvement in organization presented by Martelli's

recent edition, the *Simposio* appears as the weakest of Lorenzo's works. Its greatest defect, which has caused it to be labeled "uniform and monotonous," lies in its lengthy enumerations of the drunkards, which make up most of the poem in its extant form.[41] To do the work justice, however, it must be noted that its real variety consists in its allusions, both to literary tradition and to living personages. It is probable that reminiscences of both types, which pass unnoticed by the modern reader, would have had strong comic effect for Lorenzo's contemporaries. In writing this poem, Lorenzo was certainly not concerned with posterity. As in the *Uccellagione*, he was writing of the life around him to amuse the friends around him.[42] Narrating in the first person, he presents an account of a reality familiar to all, through equally familiar literary forms, and he distorts both to achieve a comic effect. Like the *Uccellagione*, the poem presupposes for its full appreciation an audience of initiates.

Even without reference to its topicality and to its intended audience, the work presents certain positive traits worthy of note. Lorenzo's ability to adapt traditional elements to his own purposes reveals an uncommon inventiveness and verve. His command of verse, along with his ability to manipulate his native language to achieve a desired effect, are readily apparent. The opening stanzas, which begin with the trees losing their leaves in autumn and pass to the peasant who, in that season, is anxious for the harvest, recall the beginning of the *Uccellagione* in setting a wider stage; they show a similar poetic sensitivity, and the ability to respond to nature and to relate it intimately to human activity.

Lorenzo's verbal agility also counters much of the monotony of the enumerations. There are some truly comic touches, particularly in conception, such as the story of the rector of Stia who sets out in search of his lost thirst armed with dried meat, a herring, cheese, sausage, and four anchovies tied by a string (VIII, 16–19). And perhaps the most constant impression of the poem is that in it the poet is amusing himself—with reality as he observes it in his own city, with his language, and with his own poetic tradition. As De Robertis puts it, his attitude toward reality is translated into a literary amusement.[43] And in this freshness, this genuine amusement, we find much of Lorenzo's originality.

III   The Nencia da Barberino

According to many students of Lorenzo's poetry, the *Nencia de Barberino* is clearly his masterpiece. This poem, whose entire content is a shepherd's wandering thoughts of his love for Nencia, a girl from his village, enjoyed great and immediate popularity, and was imitated by a number of other poems on similar themes. While reflecting a specific reality, it is also universal in its appeal. However, while many of Lorenzo's works have benefited from a re-evaluation in the light of modern criticism, attention to the *Nencia* has focused primarily on the question of authorship. At present, with this question at least tentatively resolved in Lorenzo's favor, the work itself may again receive the critical attention which it merits.

As in the case with almost all of Lorenzo's works, there is no autograph manuscript of the *Nencia*. The poem was first attributed to Lorenzo by Varchi in his *Ercolano* of 1560, and included among his works in the Florentine edition of 1568. Until 1907, only one version, in fifty octaves, was known; in that year, a second version of twenty octaves was found, and this has since been considered the "real" or "original" *Nencia*. In 1934, Patetta discovered a third version of the poem, which differed significantly from the previously known versions, and he was led to assert first a "collective" origin in the Medici *brigata*, then a "popular" origin based on the evidence of the several short songs and poems on the subject. The difficulty in determining both the authentic text and its origin is particularly acute with this poem, because popular mentions are abundant, and in literary texts on the subject we have several vernacular variations, an eclogue and two Latin epistles by Bartolomeo Scala, and a parody of that work in Luigi Pulci's *Beca da Dicomano*.[44]

Those favoring the so-called popular origin point to the poem's meter, the octave, long used in popular poetry; the *Nencia* so closely approximates even the tone of that poetry that some have pronounced it merely a collection of *strambotti* or *rispetti* linked by a single subject and title. But others have demonstrated that the *Nencia* of twenty octaves, that considered the "real" *Nencia*, is clearly the work of an educated author who, while able to appreciate the life of the country folk, nonetheless conveys also his detachment from it.[45] Given the popular nature of the subject, the controlling hand of an author is evident in the manner in which the various popular components are combined. The affinity with the popular tradition may in itself explain the other versions, since the poem lent itself to loose transmission through recitation and song as well as in written form.[46]

Other scholars, convinced by Patetta's arguments, denied the poem to Lorenzo and declared it the composition of a series of improvisors, each one elaborating and amplifying the work of his predecessor; this theory of a collective origin in the Medici *brigata*, however, is now widely disputed.[47] As Toschi explains, while there can be little doubt that the poem reflects the atmosphere of the group's activity, there must nonetheless be one individual who begins the poem, who sets the tone and the example.[48] It is true that even if one rejects the theories of collective and popular origin in favor of a single author, the identity of that individual cannot on present evidence be conclusively determined. I. Marchetti produced his own candidate for the authorship, Bernardo Giambullari, and began a debate that is still not ended.[49] But many indications point to Lorenzo's authorship, and more and more scholars now accept Toschi's conclusion that the "inventor and promotor and first author" was Lorenzo.[50]

While collective authorship cannot account for the highly artistic and unified nature of the poem, the influence of the group on its composition is of great importance. De Robertis finds in all of the literary Nencia versions "a small tradition of taste and a sort of collaboration,"[51] and the date of the *Nencia*, too, suggests a connection with Lorenzo's *brigata*. A ballad on the subject dated 1470 presupposes both the *Nencia* and the *Beca da Dicomano* which parodies it, thus establishing that the poem belongs to that early period of Lorenzo's life when he was frequently in the company of the *brigata* and when he also wrote, with the members of that group in mind, both the *Uccellagione* and the *Simposio*.[52]

As a literary work, the *Nencia* presents even more important similarities to the *Simposio* and the *Uccellagione*. In creating the settings in the opening stanzas of those poems, Lorenzo draws upon carefully observed moments in the life of the peasants. In the *Simposio*, the description of autumn is in terms not only of nature but also of the human activity characteristic of the season, when the peasant takes account of the results of his labor and sees "whether the past year has been such as to make him expect either happiness or future ills" (II, 7–9). Similarly, in the *Uccellagione* the activities of the country folk are described with the coming of the new day, with the peasant returning to his work and the country girl opening the door for the sheep and pigs (3–6). In both instances, these moments in the life of the peasants are used to set the stage for a different kind of activity, on a very different social level: in the case of the *Uccellagione*, for the sport of a noble "leisure class," and in the *Simposio* for the city-oriented haste of the group of drunkards. The *Nencia*, by far the most successful and interesting of the three works, now focuses on the country folk themselves. They move to the foreground and become the subject.

In the *Nencia*, as in the *Uccellagione* and in the *Simposio*, the narration is in the first person, and the narrator participates in the action of the poem. But here the essential difference of the *Nencia* from the other works is most important. In the *Uccellagione*, the narrator is a participant in the hunt, but within the fiction he remains primarily an observer; he records his motive for composing the narrative as an account of the day's sport for an absent companion. In the *Simposio*, too, the narrator is primarily an observer, and participates only to the extent that his curiosity and questions elicit the story, or stories, of the drunkards who pass by, his relation to the reader being again essentially that of a reporter. In the *Nencia*, on the other hand, the narrator becomes the central figure, the protagonist. The real subject matter of the poem is his emotion. He is not deliberately preparing an account, nor is he even aware of an audience. His presentation instead takes the form of a spontaneous outburst, occasioned by nothing other than the need to express his love; rather than to any presumed audience, he speaks to his absent Nencia, or to himself.

Because the narrator has become the protagonist, and a humble protagonist far removed from Lorenzo's own state, the question of the author's attitude again assumes major importance. The general effect of Vallera's amorous lament is indisputably comic, and some have concluded that Lorenzo is making fun of Nencia's admirer in his peasant rudeness.[53] It is obvious throughout that Lorenzo is indeed laughing at Vallera, and inviting the reader to laugh with him. The enamored shepherd's down-to-earth expressions of his love, and particularly his descriptions of Nencia, can hardly be intended as other than comic by the poem's author: "Her lips look red as coral: and inside there are two rows of teeth, that are whiter than a horse's; on both sides she has more than twenty" (IV, 1–4). But the question of the type of laughter remains. While the reader may laugh with Lorenzo at Vallera's expense, the poet does not treat his character with disdain; on the contrary, he is fundamentally in sympathy with the luckless shepherd. Lorenzo had observed the life of the country folk closely, and knew it well; furthermore, as the opening stanzas of the *Uccellagione* and the *Simposio* demonstrate, there was an affinity of feeling which made him responsive to even the more routine patterns of their existence.

The key to this attitude lies in the fact that the comic exaggerations are phrased by Vallera himself, to express his own feelings. He is seen both from within, in the intensity of his sentiment, and from without, from the perspective of the author's amused observation. The comic nature of his declarations is modified by the perceptiveness with which his psychology is suggested, and the form which they take is consistent with his down-to-earth character. It is no doubt true that not even the rudest of peasants would seriously compare his love's teeth to those of a horse in order to describe her beauty, and through the use of such exaggerations Lorenzo is obviously establishing a comic distance between personage and reader.[54] Yet Vallera, while comic in the expression of his love, is never himself a caricature. He is a man expressing passion; the strength and sincerity of that passion, while not diminishing the comic effect, qualify it for the reader.

Lorenzo succeeds in the difficult task of being detached and sympathetic at the same time, and in provoking this same ambivalence in the reader, through the sense of independent existence he establishes for his characters. One must refer to "characters" in the plural, for although only Vallera speaks, Nencia too comes to life for the reader. Her portrait, as painted by her luckless admirer, is unforgettable, to the extent that "to look like Nencia" became a common term of reference.[55] When her eyes are described as "with those lashes which seem a festivity when she raises them," the use of the demonstrative "those" instead of "some" or the possessive "her" accomplishes both the complicity of the reader and a demonstration of Vallera's psychological state. In more unconventional detail, we are told also that "she has a dimple in the middle of her chin that makes her whole face pretty." But the most striking description is that of Nencia dancing, presented directly and with charming detail:

> She is really fine at dancing,
> for she leaps like a young goat:
> turns about like a mill wheel
> and claps her hand to her little shoe.
> When she finishes the dance, she bows,
> then she turns and skips two steps,
> and she makes prettier curtsies
> than any fair citizen of Florence. (VIII, 1–8)

In this passage, Lorenzo's gift for capturing the essential feeling of a moment is obvious. The use of the diminutives "little goat" or "kid" and "little shoe," the humble but vivid comparison to the millwheel, the self-conscious little bow at the end of the dance all create the impression of being drawn from life, a direct representation of dancing seen and remembered. Without a single term of psychological reference, and through only the adoring eyes of Vallera on whom no detail is lost, the description also provides an insight into the nature of the girl, one of irrepressible good spirits. This exuberance, in its thoughtless contrast to Vallera's own state, increases both his love and his lament.

Because Vallera's delight in thinking of Nencia is mingled

with suffering, the poem is not merely a collection of stanzas in praise of the girl. It contains its own small internal drama, and its small measure of action. While Vallera suffers from his passion for her, Nencia goes her carefree way, and the poor shepherd is all too painfully aware that her charms do not have their effect on him alone: "whoever she looks at, has to fall in love," he complains, and to add to his troubles, "she has a heart hard as a stone; and she always has a thousand admirers following, all captured by those eyes" (V, 1–6). She is not merely unresponsive; it seems to Vallera that she delights in his misery. He explains in stanza 14 that having been unable to sleep the night before, he had left his bed and remained outside until the setting of the moon. When he had seen Nencia emerge from her hut with sheep and dog, he had driven his flocks in the same direction and hastened ahead to wait for her, but she had disappointed his hopes by turning back. In the final stanza, able to wait no longer, he announces that he must bid her farewell in order to care for his flock.

This final stanza of farewell exemplifies the art with which the poem is constructed:

> My little lily, you go with God,
> for my animals are nearing home.
> I wouldn't want through my diversion
> any one of them to remain in pasture.
> I see that they have crossed the river,
> and I hear Masa calling me.
> Stay happy: I go away singing
> and calling Nencia always in my heart.

The fifty-stanza version of the poem has a final section, essentially the same through the first six lines, that concludes with "Go with God, for I'm hurrying away, for I hear Nanni who wants to press the grapes"—final lines apparently inconsistent with the rest of the poem in the seeming ease with which Nencia is abandoned.[56] But in Lorenzo's poem, the stanza cited above forms a perfect conclusion. The real subject matter throughout has been, not Nencia herself, but the enamored Vallera. Throughout, he has appeared in his own setting, expressing his feelings in his own rustic language. He has hoped to join Nencia in tending the flocks, but he has been disappointed, and now he cannot wait any longer. He is not the pastoral hero of an idyll or an eclogue; his flocks will not wait while he laments his love; the day's work must be done, and Vallera and his Nencia do not live in a pastoral world. The fact that the shepherd must leave the place where he might have seen Nencia adds poignancy to his lament, and its words are effective in their simplicity, especially his wish that she "stay happy." He sees Nencia as happy, and the word evokes both the vivid images of her dancing and those of her with her own group. It also heightens the sense of Vallera's own emotion, because her gaiety and carefree attitude are the opposite of his own suffering, yet he hopes for her that they continue. Vallera, despite his attention to his tasks, will continue to call out to her in his heart, just as he has been calling out to her throughout the poem. The final episode is thus integrated into the pattern of his life and consistent with his character, and the poem's unity remains that of his feelings for Nencia.

Lorenzo's achievement in this poem lies partly in his ability to portray a character so different from himself, to describe with obvious sympathy and understanding a lifestyle so fundamentally different from his own—to convince us of the reality of Vallera. This is accomplished in part through his choice of detail. For example, when Vallera cannot sleep, he tells us: "and then I had to get out of bed: I settled under the porch of the bakehouse, and there I stayed more than an hour and a half" (XIV, 5–8). A traditional love-poet would hardly refer to such a duration as "an hour and a half" to define a vigil of love; in the matter-of-fact mind of Vallera, however, it seems entirely at home, and conveys, more clearly than a more poetic expression, not only the effects of his passion, but also the sense of bewilderment which these produce in his unaccustomed thoughts.

Remaining always within the range of plausibility in terms of Vallera's range of experience, Lorenzo presents a complex emotion. Vallera's attitude toward Nencia is by turns tender, proud, reproachful, pleading, despairing, and coaxing. From a description of her charms he passes to a description of the sad state to which they have reduced him ("they have tangled me up so much inside that I don't have the strength to eat a mouthful"), and he recovers to express his pride in her and to claim that she is the equal of anyone: "she could go as model among a thousand pretty city ladies, for she makes a good showing among the people, with her pretty actions and sweet little words" (VII, 1–4), and when she dances, as we have seen, she makes as fair a curtsy "as any fair citizen of Florence." Vallera does not deceive himself. In such passages he demonstrates that he is fully aware of his own social state, and of Nencia's as well; it is because she would be scorned by city standards that he insists on the comparison, because he is eager to take her part. Some critics have seen caricature in "the pretended poetic vein of the rude peasant, who has the illusion that he is inspired by Apollo,"[57] but there is no evidence in the poem that Vallera takes his own song so seriously. His "poetic vein," though rough, is quite genuine.

Vallera then introduces a thought that has led some critics to reproach him (and his author) for excessive sensuality.[58]

> He'll really call himself lucky
> who marries such a pretty wife;
> he'll really think luck is with him
> who has that cornflower without leaves;
> he'll really think he's blessed and happy
> and all his desires will be fulfilled,
> to have that face, and see it in his arms,
> so soft and white. (X, 1–8)

But while the effect may be sensual, the passage is not intended for that effect.[59] It is true that Vallera's passion is never spiritualized, and that his descriptions of Nencia focus on the physical, but he insists that she is "honorable" and "carefully brought up." The passage gives evidence of Vallera's direct mind, and of the strength of his desire. The reader is made party to his thoughts, and it is not surprising, since his thoughts are constantly of Nencia and his love for her, that they should lead him to consider the possibility of possessing her. The same sort of detail appears, but with obvious innocence, when he expresses his intent to go to Florence on Saturday and buy something for her there. Almost three stanzas are devoted to suggestions of trinkets she might like, included not to be comic in their humble nature or their triviality, but presented as Vallera's mind eagerly visualizes each of them.

Lorenzo's success in presenting this range of feeling while maintaining the impression of spontaneity is due in part to his facility with language, his ability to adopt the peasant turn of phrase and to render the savor of rustic speech. Rochon notes that in the *Nencia* the use of this speech is not at all the literary game later writers would make of it; in Lorenzo's poem it is a reflection of his deep feeling for these people, deliberately used to create an impression of life.[60]

During twenty stanzas consisting entirely of Vallera's talk of Nencia, the poet manages to avoid monotony, and this seemingly spontaneous variety is far from artless. The most obvious evidence of its careful development occurs halfway through the poem, when Vallera is so overcome by his feelings that he begins to address Nencia directly, as if she were present: "If you knew, Nencia, the great love that I bear for your beautiful shining eyes," and he continues to address her for the rest of the poem, until the final stanza when he takes his leave of her. This change in no way appears artificial, a manipulation of the narration to achieve variety; it is the strength of Vallera's desire for Nencia's presence that conjures up the figure of the girl before his mind, and this in turn introduces the use of direct address in a completely natural way. It is an indication of Lorenzo's poetic achievement in creating a reality for Nencia as seen only through the eyes of Vallera that some critics describe a number of Vallera's imagined actions with her as if they were actually carried out in her presence: pleading with her, promising her ornaments, questioning her about the size of the stones for the necklace he proposes to give her.[61]

Even more important in achieving the effect of spontaneity and avoiding monotony in the narrative is the use of what is essentially a stream-of-consciousness technique. The direction of the poem is determined by the direction of Vallera's thoughts: a description of Nencia's charms results in a cry of pain, which leads to a report of his having suffered sleepless through the previous night, and of his attempt to join her in the morning; this thought of meeting her is followed, directed by his desire to find something to please her, by his mental enumeration of all the things he might buy for her in the city. Sometimes he addresses her as if they are on intimate terms, calling her "my Nencia" or "my little Nencia," and in the final stanza, "my little lily"; he imagines her asking him for some trinket, or at other times he is most aware of her unresponsiveness and distance. The past and the future mingle freely with images of the present, and even the reality of the present is seldom clearly defined, as all of Vallera's thoughts are with Nencia, who never appears on the scene.

Lorenzo, then, is clearly guided in the *Nencia* by his appreciation and observation of country life. But even in this, perhaps the most original of his works, he draws freely upon literary tradition. Much of the humor presupposes a lettered audience. The first stanza, beginning "I burn with love, and I must sing for a lady who consumes my heart," introduces the subject of the poem in a manner not inconsistent with spiritualized love-poetry in the Italian mode. But the second stanza, again using poetic reminiscences, transposes it to the level of the peasant, when the love-sick Vallera enumerates the places which he has visited without finding the equal of his Nencia. The listing of towns recalls a famous poem by the Sicilian poet Cielo d'Alcamo; but while Cielo relates that he visited Calabria, Tuscany, Lombardy, Puglia, and Constantinople, the poor Vallera boasts of visits to the tiny towns of the Mugello region, in which he found, not only no girl to equal his Nencia, but also no market to equal that of his native Barberino.[62] The juxtaposition of the two stanzas contributes to the comic effect, but only for those familiar with the tradition of the first. Similarly, many of Vallera's exaggerations in his declarations of love and in his descriptions of Nencia acquire an extra dimension of humor from their thinly veiled allusions to the more exaggerated love-poetry written in Lorenzo's own time.[63]

In a more serious literary vein, Lorenzo also makes use of the eclogue. Vallera is not really a peasant, but a shepherd, although he lives in the Mugello valley and not on the exalted slopes of Mount Partenio; and like the Corinto of Lorenzo's poem of that name, he loves, and sings of his love.[64] In the *Nencia* Lorenzo adapts some of the basic conceptions of the eclogue to his less idealized context, and at the same time, he adapts the popular forms of rustic song.[65] While the eclogue and rustic song are far distant in style and literary level, he utilizes their basic affinity as the basis for his own poem, and in this particular sense the *Nencia* is an achievement that has no parallel in his period.

Study of the *Nencia* demonstrates, then, that while Lorenzo is well versed in his own literary tradition, he is in no way awed by it. Drawing upon it freely, he adapts to his own purposes whatever elements contribute to the chosen treatment of his subject, and all are subordinated to the presentation of Vallera. In both subject and presentation, the *Nencia* illustrates the independence that so frequently characterizes Lorenzo's poetry.

CHAPTER 4

The Poetry of Love and its Interpretation

LORENZO wrote a large number of lyric poems, most of them in sonnet form. The entire collection includes 108 sonnets, 8 *canzoni*, 5 *sestine*, and a single ballad, all almost exclusively devoted to the subject of love. Forty-one of his sonnets are combined within the definite prose context of the *Comento ad alcuni dei sonetti* (commentary to some of his own sonnets). Unlike Petrarch's collection of poems in his *Canzoniere*, however, which contains Lorenzo's most obvious models, the collection of the *Rime* suggests no clear relation between its various poems in either subject or date of composition.[1]

There is ample evidence that Lorenzo was considered precocious in his composition of love lyrics. While most of the poems are of uncertain date, his earliest poetic efforts have been dated with certainty as early as 1465, and he continued to compose poetry of this type throughout his life, so that the *rime* are the major element of continuity in his poetic activity.[2]

The lyrics in the collection are generally of two types: those in the Petrarchan manner, and those in which the influence of the earlier *stil nuovo* poets predominates. The earlier poems are generally of the first, Petrarchan, type; Bigi concludes from his study of Lorenzo's lyrics that this earlier manner was primary until 1476–77.[3] Most of the sonnets included in the *Comento*, however, reflect the later stilnovistic influence, and may in this sense indicate the same increased appreciation of the earlier poetic tradition found in the defense of the vernacular poets in the *Epistola* to Frederic of Aragon and in the compilation of the *Raccolta aragonese*.[4] Despite the highly derivative nature of almost all of Lorenzo's lyrics, his contemporaries generally considered them his major literary achievement.

I *The* Rime

Throughout the collection of the *Rime,* the element of direct imitation is the most obvious characteristic of the poems. In the works of both the early Petrarchan and the later stilnovistic styles, however, the degree of imitation varies greatly, as does the poetic effect. Some of the poems of the earlier manner are no more than obvious exercises in the popular Petrarchan mode, while others, although utilizing both the vocabulary and the form of Petrarch's poetry, nonetheless reveal an element of personal inspiration and an independent poetic achievement.

The influence of Petrarch's *Canzoniere* is unmistakable in the *Rime.* Fundamental imitation of both concept and technique is illustrated by the second poem in Lorenzo's collection, the poetic account of the occasion when he was first bound by love. In Lorenzo's poem and in the Petrarchan sonnet that serves as its model (*Canz.* 3), the description of the event is essentially the same, with both poets captured by the lady's glance, but the verses of preparation are characteristically different. Petrarch begins with a brief indication that the day was Good Friday, but proceeds at once to the statement of his new bondage. In Lorenzo's sonnet, eight verses are devoted to the identification of the season as that of spring; while his first verse recalls that of Petrarch ("it was the time when . . ."), the lengthy description of the season contributes only a decorative setting with no significance for the emotional event that is the poem's subject. Petrarch was surprised by love's victory because his thoughts were only of the day of general sorrow; Lorenzo was surprised because he "would not have been afraid even if Hercules had returned to life." While the various elements of Petrarch's poem contribute to a single effect of interiorization and subdued emotional tension, presenting not only the fact of his love and its occasion, but also implications of its significance, Lorenzo's sonnet lacks a central focus.

While Lorenzo draws freely upon the entire body of Petrarch's poetry for both concept and phrase, occasionally one of his sonnets is a deliberate and consistent imitation of a single, clearly identifiable poem from the *Canzoniere.* Sonnet 8 is such an imitation of Petrarch's famous sonnet (189) based on the single metaphor of the poet's ship tossed by a storm. Lorenzo's sonnet again fails to equal the effectiveness of its model. In Petrarch's poem, "la nave mia" (my boat) is the symbol of the poet himself, and the storm is that of his conflicting thoughts and emotions, over which he despairs of asserting control. The poem is a metaphorical projection of the inner tempest on the outer world. It is the concrete image of a ship tossed at sea, however, which underlies the development of this concept in Lorenzo's poem: the poet himself appears more as a passenger in a ship beset by adversity. This contrast is particularly apparent as each poet describes those who control his course: Petrarch's "at each oar a ready thought and wild" is replaced in Lorenzo's poem with "Fortune and Love at the rudder." While Petrarch fears these thoughts themselves, Fortune and Love point out to Lorenzo that it is useless to fear, assuring him that "it is better to hope in every adversity." The contrast is completed in the concluding verses of each poem: Petrarch's closing note is one of quiet desperation, with reason and art dead amid the waves, so that he begins to despair of reaching port, while Lorenzo's poem closes with the poet's optimistic and sententious acceptance of the advice offered him by Fortune and Love: "and it seems to be still true, that he who endures at last overcomes."

The extreme forms of imitation of technique, particularly the abuse of antitheses that characterized much of Renaissance Petrarchism, are fortunately few in the *Rime*.[5] As De Robertis points out, however, Lorenzo at his best sought in Petrarch not merely a literary model, but an exercise in clarity and a means of inner discovery, and he occasionally succeeds in recreating the Petrarchan experience on his own terms.[6] One of the best examples of this success is the effective presentation of sonnet 36, labelled in the manuscript, "sonnet written while going along the seashore in Maremma." The Petrarchan poems that serve as models (especially *Canz.* 35) present the poet seeking out the most deserted routes, but finding that even in deepest solitude love walks still at his side. Lorenzo's variation on this theme is characteristic in its emphasis on action; when he seeks out rough and deserted paths and abandons society to find "the habitation of the beasts of the forest," it is to determine whether he cannot escape his preoccupation with love through new sights and

experiences: "whether the soul may be calmed and quieted by
new things." When he concludes that he cannot escape the
"sweet pain" of his love, it is because his imagination presents
him with his lady wherever he turns on that ancient shore:
"I see her there amid the leaves, a new Diana"; "it seems to me
that she takes away her kingdom from Thetis." In these images
the recreated world of myth, the same world that furnishes the
inspiration for his several poems on mythological subjects,
combines intimately with the world of his own reality to create
an atmosphere of sentiment and suggestion peculiar to Lorenzo.

Sonnet 83, addressed to the violets, is a more celebrated
example of Lorenzo's originality: "Oh beautiful violet, you were
born there where my first desire began; tears both sad and
beautiful were the waters which nurtured and bathed you more
than once." His lady, having cared for the flowers, had sent
them to the poet as a gift; knowing that they would prefer to
return to their donor, he keeps them close to the place where
his heart had been until it had abandoned him to seek his lady's
company. This is the third of three poems about the violets in
the Rime, and the subject was treated also by other poets of the
day; Lorenzo himself presents it again in Sonnet 16 of the
Comento, where it is accompanied by a long explanation of the
gift and its significance.[7] These sonnets, while clearly Petrarchan
in style and development, are not primarily imitative. In them
an episode of Lorenzo's experience, or at least a context that
has imaginative validity for him, lends a note of freshness and
genuine feeling.

The poems of Lorenzo's later style, including most of the
sonnets of the Comento, are as varied as those of his Petrarchan
manner. The imitation is sometimes mechanical and formal,
using all of the conventions and rhetoric of the stilnovistic
style.[8] But in these poems, too, he sometimes recaptures the
spirit as well as the form of the earlier poetry.[9]

One poem in the Rime marks a clear and radical departure
from either the Petrarchan or the stilnovistic models. This is
the famous sonnet 50, "to the Duke of Calabria in the name of
a lady," whose originality is immediately apparent in the fact
that the poem's voice is that of the lady herself.[10] The poem is
intensely realistic; its love is not the idealized sentiment of the

earlier poetic tradition, in which the lady is loved from a distance, but rather an openly physical relationship in which she is not only possessed but subsequently abandoned. The expression of her sentiment is subtle and complex, beginning with a strong reproach to her lover—"It was enough to take away my liberty, and lead me away from my chaste life"—and then softening with the admission of her continuing love, such that only her memory of former happiness keeps death from ending her present sorrow. The simplicity of the poem's vocabulary and its carefully controlled modulation of tone create an effect of intense emotion, and the characteristically Petrarchan expressions of her "sweet martyrdom" and "sad delight" appear as completely natural expressions of bittersweet emotions in recalling her love. The poem is highly original not only within the context of the *Rime,* but with regard to the entire poetic tradition of Lorenzo's time. It is also the collection's incontestable evidence that its author's poetic talent far exceeded that of skillful imitation.

Critical judgment of the *Rime* has ranged from general condemnation of the lyrics as wholly derivative and artificial, to praise of their personal sentiment and their appreciation of nature.[11] De Sanctis declared that not a single poem could be called truly perfect, nor was there a single poem that did not contain something of merit.[12] It is obvious from the collection that Lorenzo did not write Petrarchan sonnets as well as Petrarch; nor did he generally equal the best of the stilnovistic poets on their own terms. Occasionally, however, he finds his own poetic voice, and the resulting lyrics merit comparison with any of his day.

II   *The* Comento ad alcuni dei suoi sonetti

Lorenzo's *Comento,* perhaps the most ambitious of his literary efforts, is more complex than its title suggests. The forty-one sonnets and their frequently lengthy prose presentations are arranged into a sequence based on the theme of love, and preceded by a prologue of several pages in which Lorenzo advances a justification of his work on several counts. The treatment of the theme of love is itself complex: in the sonnets love is considered in general and in particular, in its origins, its symptoms, and its effects, while from the prose explanations emerges a psychology and a philosophy of love reflecting both the early Italian poetic tradition from Dante to Petrarch, and the contemporary interpretation of Platonic doctrine as elaborated by Marsilio Ficino.

Of the serious critical problems presented by the work, the simplest is that it is not certain how nearly the present version of the *Comento* approximates Lorenzo's plan. Its unfinished state is suggested not only by the fact that the final section makes no attempt to provide a conclusion for the work as a whole, but also, and more important, by the numerous inconsistencies and lacunae throughout the text itself. There are indications that Lorenzo, while perhaps intending no further additions to his material, was still reworking and reconciling its various segments at the time when the work was definitively interrupted. Martelli concludes after a detailed study that the work in its present form can be considered an amassing of material that was only beginning to take on a definite shape; it not only apparently lacks some parts, but above all lacks an ordering of the individual segments that would render the work as a whole clearly intelligible.[13]

The chronological relation between sonnets and commentary poses a related but more complex problem. The widely accepted assumption is that all, or almost all, of the poems were composed during an early period of Lorenzo's poetic activity, and that the *Comento* was undertaken at a later date to explain and relate these poems. This later date, on the basis of events of 1478–80 and perhaps 1481 referred to in some of the poems, and on the evidence of a well-known letter from Pico della Mirandola in which Lorenzo is urged to conclude the "paraphrase" of his love lyrics, has been placed at 1482–1484.[14] There is other evidence, however, that many of the poems were accompanied by a commentary at the time of their original composition, and that these independent units were later organized into a sequence with the addition of further prose material and perhaps a few additional poems.

After a study of this material, Martelli concludes that there were three successive versions of the *Comento*. In 1473–74, he suggests, Lorenzo had already written and commented on a number of the sonnets: as he composed the poems, he would from time to time have added a gloss to those poems that seemed to him most interesting, intending to bring them together according to a logical order at a later date. The ordering of those poems referred to in Poliziano's *Nutricia* of 1486 suggests to Martelli the form assumed by Lorenzo's second redaction of the material, following closely the classical pattern of the love-episode; the reconstruction of this version according to Poliziano's references produces an extremely linear plot, which corresponds perfectly to the theory of love elaborated by Ficino. The final stage, according to Martelli's hypothesis, would have begun in the last years of Lorenzo's life, in 1490 or later, with the addition of the *proemio* and the commentary to at least one sonnet, and possible further revisions.[15]

Lorenzo's fundamental design as it emerges from the existing *Comento* is the presentation of a sequence of love-sonnets as illustrations of various moments in a personal experience of love, and the relation of the lyrics to a more universal interpretation of that experience. The model for this presentation is clearly Dante's *Convivio*, for its philosophical interpretation of a number of lyrics, and particularly his *Vita Nuova*, in which he tells in poems and in prose commentary of his youthful love for Beatrice. The poems of the *Vita Nuova* are said to have been written in direct response to the moments they describe, and the accompanying prose provides both the context and an explanation of the significance of those moments seen from a larger and later perspective. The *Vita Nuova* is very different from Lorenzo's *Comento*, however, in the relationship between the prose and the poems. Dante's commentary is itself often poetic in effect, as Garsia notes, because when the poet returns to consider the episodes described in the poems it is with an emotion frequently more intense than the emotional inspiration for the original composition.[16] The constant focus in the *Vita Nuova*, in the prose as well as in the poems, is the immediate and personal experience of love, and the subsequent interpretation of that experience serves only to clarify and heighten its significance. Lorenzo's commentary, in contrast, is generally devoid of passion; it leads away from the poems and from the experience which occasioned them, into lengthy philosophical discussions of which the poems often seem to be merely cited as illustrations.

The prose *proemio* with which the *Comento* begins addresses itself not to the introduction of the subject of the work, but rather to its justification. In this lengthy and largely independent section (pp. 297–315 in the Bigi edition), Lorenzo acknowledges and answers three objections to his commentary: the presumption of providing a commentary to his own poems; the attention to poems whose subject, love, may be considered unworthy; and the composition of the entire work in the vernacular. The importance of Lorenzo's discussion of these topics is not limited to the *Comento;* in fact the *proemio* contributes little to the understanding of the work it introduces, but it remains of major relevance to Lorenzo's literary activity as a whole.

Lorenzo dismisses the notion that it is presumptuous to comment on one's own poems by observing that the poet is himself best qualified to explain his works, since no one better than he can know his meaning or elicit its truth. Not content with this obvious point, however, Lorenzo adds a general theoretical response that is indicative of the seriousness with which he considered his literary activity. Everyone should seek to work for the benefit of mankind, he asserts, each according to his own particular ability, by putting his talents at the disposition of others; and while he himself would have desired to be useful in greater things, he nonetheless will not refuse whatever his talent and skills may offer others through the explanation of the meaning of his poetry.

The criticisms directed to the choice of love as subject are clearly not anticipated but real. Lorenzo sharply labels them "calumnies," and his summary of them reveals the personal nature of the attack: "that I have devoted time both to composing and to commenting things which are worth no effort or time at all, being amorous passions, etc., and especially among my many necessary occupations" (p. 300). In response, he undertakes a full-scale theoretical defense of love, not only asserting that it is not reprehensible, but continuing to declare it in fact an "almost necessary and quite true indication of *gentilezza* and greatness of spirit, and above all an incitement to worthy and excellent things, and to bring to effect those virtues which exist in potential in the human spirit." This is clear, he explains, to whoever understands the nature of love, for its true definition is nothing other than the appetite for beauty.[17] Its result is that all base and ugly things displease anyone who truly loves, keeping him from all the errors to which men are generally subject; furthermore, assuming that the object of his love is worthy and therefore discerning, to win her favor the lover seeks to demonstrate his own worthiness and excellence in all things. This recognition of the ennobling effect of love is attested, Lorenzo points out, by the most noted Italian poets, who wrote that love and *gentilezza* are one and the same. And to this theoretical justification he adds that of nature: man can hardly blame that which is dictated by nature, and nothing is more natural than the desire to be united with that which one finds beautiful. This desire was given to man, by nature, for his benefit—to ensure the continuation of the species through human propagation.[18]

The general argument abruptly becomes more personal. If none of these reasons be admitted, he says, the harshest judge should at least concede this small license to "the tender age of youth, which seems less subject to the censure and judgment of men, and in which no error appears so grave" (p. 304). And in his own case, Lorenzo adds, if even youth does not excuse the lover, then "compassion at least should justify me, because having been in my youth greatly persecuted both by men and by fortune, that little relief which I found only in loving fervently and in the composition and commenting of my verses should not be denied to me" (p. 306). This reference to adversities of his own life, elaborated briefly in the commentary to sonnet 10, is one of the most personal passages in all of Lorenzo's work.

In his answer to the third criticism Lorenzo defends the vernacular in a manner that recalls the *Epistola* to Frederic of Aragon. Some scorn the vernacular, he says, as neither capable nor worthy of any excellent subject. But a language is not less worthy because it is in common use, and it is rather in terms of its inherent perfection or imperfection that it must be judged. Human judgment may vary about the sweetness and harmony of the language, and its spread depends on fortune; but to be worthy

a language must be in itself copious and abundant, able to provide clear expression for the concepts of the mind. We may,
then, judge a language worthy "when in it are written subtle
things and things necessary to human life, both to our mind
and to the utility of men and their well-being" (p. 307). Applying this standard and test to the Italian vernacular, he finds that
its worthiness has been amply demonstrated by the works of
Dante, Petrarch, Boccaccio, Cavalcanti and others. Lorenzo concludes the justification of his own use of the vernacular with a
defense of his chosen form, the sonnet, as that requiring the
greatest skill.[19]

The prologue to the *Comento* is more than the author's theoretical justification of his subject, opinions, and procedure. It has
the tone of polemic, of a serious response to direct criticism
on several fronts. While the necessity for his defense of the
vernacular is obvious, the defense of love suggests a more basic
and personal effort at self-justification. Martelli bases his conclusion that the *proemio* was written near the end of Lorenzo's
life in part on the probability that the defense of love rather than
its celebration would have seemed both unnecessary and incom-
prehensible before a period beginning around 1490, the year in
which Girolamo Savonarola returned to Florence and began to
win a following that included several members of Lorenzo's
former circle. The tacit polemic between Lorenzo and his critic,
taking the form on Lorenzo's side of a cultural conflict, would
explain the tone of careful and deliberate self-justification that
pervades the entire first section.[20]

The final part of the *proemio* is a more specific defense against
possible criticism for having begun the *Comento* with a series
of sonnets occasioned by a death. This departs from tradition,
Lorenzo acknowledges, and seems almost to pervert the order
of nature, "establishing as a beginning that which in all human
things is generally the ultimate conclusion." For the appropri-
ateness of this sequence he offers a difficult philosophical
explanation, applying Aristotle's dictum of loss as the principle
of creation to the death which stands at the beginning of his
new work: "and all the more because he who examines it more
subtly, will find the beginning of the life of love to proceed
from death, because he who lives for love, first dies to other

things." As examples he cites the works of Homer, Virgil, and Dante, each of whom sends his hero first to the Inferno. Orpheus is the most suggestive example; his turning to look back, Lorenzo says, may be interpreted as an indication that he "was not truly dead, and thus had not reached the perfection of his happiness, to have his Eurydice" (p. 315). This passage remains without further elaboration; as Momigliano suggests, it appears to reflect a mystical inspiration, based perhaps on an original interpretation of the myth of Orpheus.[21] Lipari sees this section of the first four sonnets and their commentary as a key to the meaning of the *Comento,* a treatise on the concept of love found in the *dolce stil* tradition; the death of the young girl would thus represent a mystic death of the early Italian tradition and its ideal, from which a new style and a new inspiration proper to the Renaissance must be born.[22] It seems much more likely, however, that the suggestion of mystical as opposed to literal death was added by Lorenzo at a later date, while the composition of the poems themselves was inspired by an actual experience.[23]

These first four sonnets form a unit: all are presented as the poet's response to the death of a young lady for whom the entire city of Florence mourned. She is generally identified as Simonetta Cattaneo, who died in April 1476 at the age of 23.[24] Critics have sometimes misrepresented Lorenzo in assuming that he here suggests a personal love, and they have criticized the artificiality of a love occasioned by the beauty of the dead girl as she is carried in funeral procession. Lorenzo, however, makes the nature of his own involvement quite clear. In reaction to this untimely death, he explains, "all the Florentines of talent, as was fitting in such a public bereavement, variously expressed their grief, some in verse and some in prose, about the bitterness of this death, and each attempted to praise her according to his own ability; and I wished to be among them, and to accompany their tears with the sonnets which follow" (p. 316).[25]

The commentary to the first two of these sonnets offers the context and circumstances of their composition. He and a friend are speaking of the common loss when he sees a star that appears unusually bright; perhaps, he muses, the soul of the dead girl has been united with it. Then, he continues, "since it seemed to me that this thought was good material for a sonnet, I took leave of my friend, and composed the following poem." The second sonnet is similarly introduced. As he wandered alone through the meadows following the girl's death, completely absorbed in the thought and memory of her, he observed a sunflower and recalled Ovid's story that this flower had once been a girl in love with Apollo, who after her transformation still turns to follow the progress of her beloved through the heavens. This suggests to Lorenzo the greater misfortune of the human lover who loses his lady, because the flower, losing her beloved each evening, regains him each morning with the return of the sun. But if the lover has lost sight of his lady forever in this life, when he dies he will be more favored: "then his soul, freed from his body, will be able to contemplate the beauty of her soul, much more beautiful than she was while first visible to his eyes, because the light of human eyes is but a shadow relative to the light of the soul" (p. 320).

The third sonnet is introduced by a more general comment, on the melancholy that is the common nature of all lovers, from which one may judge the sorrow caused by the girl's death in those who had loved her. When Lorenzo speaks of himself in the poem as one of these, it is through an imaginative transposition into this state of deeper personal mourning, of which the poet becomes merely a representative. As he explains in the commentary, when love, the graces, and the muses all have cause to weep, whoever does not weep with them shows himself devoid of feeling. The difficulty of escaping his meditation on the common sorrow is the subject of the fourth sonnet, in which the great loss become the poet's major preoccupation. These first four sonnets with their commentary do not suggest an early love of the poet which is then quickly forgotten with the appearance of a new lady. Deeply impressed by the death and the mourning which the death occasioned, however, the poet is led through his imaginative participation in the experience of this sorrow into a meditation on death, love, and separation.

Lorenzo himself calls attention to the transition that follows these four sonnets. Since all of the poems that follow are very different, he states, they require a new argument, one which will bear out his earlier assertion that "death was appropriately the beginning of this new life," the experience of love for his own lady. While all men have a natural appetite for beauty, it is difficult to know in what it consists, so that men proceed differently in their search for it. Because of the nature of human intelligence, it is easier for man to recognize things in general than in particular, and this is the explanation of the particular function of the death-episode in his personal experience: it was for him a confused awareness of love, a general or universal recognition from which he could proceed to a particular knowledge of love through his personal experience. The two stages are directly related, he insists, because his meditation on love led him to wonder whether any other lady of his city was worthy of such love and praise. Convinced that it would be the greatest happiness to serve such a lady, he begins a deliberate search. Just as he despairs of finding one who would merit "a true and totally constant love," he is led by his friends to a public celebration—"almost against my will and, I believe, by my destiny." There he sees a lady whose beauty surpasses even that of the dead girl. Inquiring of those who know her, he satisfies himself on all counts of her delicacy, wit, and manners, and later finds her to be all that he had sought: "nothing could be desired in a beautiful and gentle woman which was not found in her in abundance" (p. 329).

At this point the poet becomes the lover, and the rest of the sonnets and their commentary are predicated on the personal experience and its interpretation. Some critics have labelled both the subject and its poetic treatment artificial because of its emphasis on the philosophical incentive to seek beauty.[26] The impulse to seek an accord between the ideal image and the real creature, however, while clearly in conformity with the major philosophy of Lorenzo's time, is not to be quickly dismissed as either artificial or insincere. In any case, the presentation of the "new life" of love as occasioned by a meditation on death is merely a poetic fiction. The lady of both the *Rime* and the *Comento* was, according to substantial contemporary evidence, Lucrezia Donati, who had already been the object of Lorenzo's love and poetry for some ten years at the time of the death of Simonetta, who inspired the opening sonnets. The sequence of death followed by life was probably superimposed at a later

date, both for poetic effect and as a more appropriate introduction to the philosophy elaborated in the *Comento*.[27]

There is, however, a clear difference between the introductory
section and the remainder of the work in the relation between
commentary and poems. After the poems on the death of the
young girl, in which the commentary serves as effective introduction, it focuses primarily on the exposition of a doctrine of
love which frequently helps little or not at all to explain the
poems thus introduced. The frequent digressions that incorporate
Lorenzo's views on many subjects are related, if only super-
ficially, by their contribution to a complex philosophy and a
psychology of love. There are frequent indications that the
philosophy rather than the poetry was Lorenzo's major concern. Sonnet 10 of the *Comento*, for example, on the theme of
the relation between Fortune and Love, was answered in verse
by three other major poets who offered diverse philosophical
interpretations of that rivalry.[28]

As Lorenzo asserts in the *proemio*, there is precedent for the
philosophical interpretation of love poetry in Dante, in the *stil
nuovo* poets, and in Petrarch, all of whom presented the poet's
love for a lady as an experience with universal implications and
an ennobling effect on the lover. From these earlier poets Lorenzo
also derives much of his vocabulary—the stress on the *gentilezza*
of the lady, for example—and the heavy use of certain conventions in describing the psychology of love, particularly the personification of the *spiritelli* or little spirits that pass from the
lady's eyes to those of the lover and thence into his heart, producing all the effects of love.[29] These borrowed elements sometimes assume a peculiarly Renaissance form in Lorenzo's poetry,
as in the concept of *gentilezza* which tends to become synony-
mous with *humanitas* and to imply a wide ideal of culture and
of refinement.[30]

The most fundamental difference between the presentations
of the love-experience in the earlier tradition and in Lorenzo's
work is that in Lorenzo's work both the human and the quasi-
divine tendencies are more pronounced.[31] This contrast of
extremes is most evident in his *Selve d'Amore*, where the lady
appears briefly as a human lover but is transformed at the conclusion into a highly spiritualized, essentially pagan goddess of

spring. In the *Comento*, however, the heightening of the human element is most pronounced. Even Lorenzo's theoretical argument of the ennobling effect of love is no longer couched in the largely spiritualized concepts of the *stil nuovo* or of Petrarch. Not content with the Platonic definition of love as the appetite for beauty, he sets two conditions for a worthy love—that it be for one person alone, and that it be constant—and reconciles these with the philosophical definition in clear and notably realistic terms. It is necessary for the perfection of love that the lady have many worthy qualities in addition to her beauty, he insists, because while love is both of the eyes and of beauty, the other qualities ensure its continuation: physical beauty may be diminished or destroyed by infirmity or age, but these other qualities remain no less welcome to the spirit and the heart than beauty had been to the eyes (pp. 301–302).

Most important is the requirement that this ennobling love be reciprocal—the major difference between Lorenzo's ideal of love and that of the stilnovistic tradition and Petrarch.[32] The insistence that the highest love necessarily presupposes reciprocity appears not only in the theoretical statement of the *proemio* but also in the development of the story of love that emerges from the sonnets and their commentary. Lorenzo's lady returns his love, and experiences its joy and pain. Rather than a distant love divided into two phases by the lady's death, the basic story presented by both Dante and Petrarch, Lorenzo's love is punctuated by absences regretted by both himself and the lady, and by the attempt to reconcile an ideal of love with the complexities of a real relationship.

In most of this, Lorenzo follows Ficino. While the *Comento* merits Bigi's label of being "ostentatiously erudite,"[33] drawing heavily and openly on a variety of sources, it is Ficino's *Sopra lo Amore*, in turn a commentary on Plato's *Simposio*, which furnishes the fundamental interpretation of love. It was almost surely Ficino's work that suggested to Lorenzo the compatibility of stilnovistic tendencies with Neoplatonic philosophy.[34] In this philosophy as expounded by Ficino, human beauty incites in man the desire for continual elevation and perfection. But torment is an inevitable concomitant of this process, for as beauty is increasingly manifest, the desire to enjoy it also becomes more intense. Martelli sees as the characteristic feature of this philosophy of love "the affirmation that in the heart of the lover there coexist at all times possession and non-possession, pain and joy, hope and fear."[35] This tension, which is characteristic of much of Lorenzo's poetry, finds its most direct expression in the Comento.

In the Comento, the intuitive force of this perception is often replaced by a rigid schematization of the stages of love and their development, resulting in philosophical digressions that not only add little to the sonnet they introduce, but in fact detract from the effectiveness of the poetry itself.[36] Even when focusing on the poems, these schema tend to emphasize their prose values, the total explanation of discourse and of idea.[37] This tendency is illustrated by the commentary to sonnet 39, in which the lover describes the pallor of his lady's face when they meet unexpectedly. The poem lacks neither lovely images nor genuine feeling: the sudden pallor heightens the beauty of her face as the green grass emphasizes that of the flower, or as the color of the clear sky makes the stars more beautifully distinct. The effect is undermined by the following two verses which quite unnecessarily explain the comparison, but the original images reveal an intimate sense of the relation between the beauty of a human face and the beauty of nature. The commentary, however, leads immediately away from the poem, beginning with an exposition of science and ignorance as the extreme degrees of human understanding asserted by Plato, with opinion, which may or may not be accurate, as the intermediate stage. This introduces a lengthy passage on the relativity of most human judgments, so that, for example, a man is considered tall or short only in relation to the average height of men. The poet explains that this introduction was necessary because his sonnet "deals with the supreme beauty which came to the face of my lady through a chance which in others usually diminishes beauty, and in her only multiplied it," and after relating the circumstances of their meeting, he continues with an unimaginative and detailed explanation of the comparisons on which the sonnet is based. The impetus of the poem, an immediate esthetic perception, is lost in the detailed explanation.

Lorenzo's prose style in these long passages of commentary,

praised by Spongano for its relative freedom from the latinisms that characterized much of the vernacular prose of the century,[38] is dominated by his heavily philosophical preoccupation. Fubini points out that while perhaps unusually free of latinisms, the prose of the *Comento* labors under the greater weight of scholastic argument, to which the author consciously submits. This is most obvious in the insistence on certain stylistic formulas, and particularly in the prevalence of such phrases as "it necessarily follows that"; "and if this be the case, it must be that"; and "he who examines the question finds that."[39]

This judgment of Lorenzo's commentary is even more clearly illustrated by the contrast of those few passages in which the prose itself is lyrical and serves to enhance the sonnet. In one of the most celebrated, the poet describes the month of April. The sonnet is placed between two others presenting the poet's lady as a "new Flora," who by her beauty and her very presence calls forth all the beauty of spring. The commentary, beginning with the realistic context of the "common custom" of Florentine families to leave the city in April in order to enjoy that most beautiful time in their country villas, reports that Lorenzo's lady was among those who went away. He imagines her then bringing the season to full beauty and harmony through her presence and through her voice. While the effect is dissipated in a detailed discussion of Plato's concept of musical harmony, the passage relevant to the sonnets presents, as Fubini comments, "a humanistic springtime, in which the pleasure of the new season is mingled with that of the lovely rhythms and expressions, in which the prose assumes a poetic character superior to that of the sonnets which it proposes to explain."[40]

While not all the *Comento* can be dismissed as "no more and no less than a decorous exercise,"[41] much of its philosophical discussion does appear dry, uninspired, and irrelevant to the sonnets. If, as seems likely, Lorenzo composed the *proemio* and substantially revised other parts of the commentary during a period near the end of his life, when he felt his love poetry and perhaps his poetic activity in general to be under attack as frivolous and unworthy, the *Comento* may well offer not the interpretation and explanation of his sonnets, which he claims, but rather a reinterpretation, which forces the poems to bear the weight of a continuous philosophical presentation for which they were not originally intended. In any case, when put together the pieces of the *Comento* produce an effect of fragmentation in which poems and prose do not function effectively together. The most successful sections, notably the *proemio* and the first four sonnets with their commentary, form a clear contrast to the remainder of the work, and despite the considerable interest of these and other occasional passages of real beauty, the impression remains that the work fails to realize its author's ambitious goal.

CHAPTER 5

The Claims of Youth and Pleasure

LORENZO as poet is perhaps best known for his carnival songs, and the famed *Canzone di Bacco,* with its uninhibited urging of the enjoyment of the present moment, is often cited as his most characteristic work. His celebration of carefree pleasure, however, makes up only a small part of his literary production. Other works, including the *Nencia da Barberino* and most of the mythological poems as well as parts of the *Rime* and the *Comento,* reflect his appreciation of earthly pleasures, but within a different frame of reference; only the festival poems and the *novelle* of *Giacoppo* and *Ginevra* take the defense of youth and pleasure as their theme.

The festival poems and the short stories are very different in type. The poems, which include both dance songs and carnival pieces, are popular in their inspiration. The short stories, whose attribution to Lorenzo has only recently been confirmed, are an exercise in a well-established literary form, reflecting the influence of the prose tradition of the *novelle* and patterned on the stories of Boccaccio. Their thematic similarities, however, are more important. Both defend the claims of youth to enjoy the present—in the festival pieces because youth vanishes quickly, in the story of *Giacoppo* in terms of the natural attraction of two young people whose union is prevented by an unsuitable marriage. In the poems time is the major enemy, and youth in general is celebrated, while a single unfortunate marriage is the focus of the plot in the story. In both, Lorenzo's sympathies are on the side of youth and pleasure.

I *The Festival Poems*

To those familiar with the masterpieces of Italian literature, mention of Lorenzo de'Medici as poet immediately recalls the refrain of the *Canzone di Bacco,* the "Song of Bacchus":

Oh, how beautiful is youth,
that is fleeing all the same!
Let him who wishes to, be gay:
There's no certainty about tomorrow.[1]

The melody and spontaneous vigor of these verses have guaranteed the lasting fame of Lorenzo's celebration of the spirit of Carnival. This poem, probably the best-known of Lorenzo's works and often termed the most representative and most successful, forms part of a large and varied group of carnival pieces containing the distinct types of the *canzoni a ballo* (dance songs) and the *canti carnascialeschi* (carnival songs).

The *canzone a ballo* is a poetic descendant of the ballad, a form which, in its popular origin, involved the combination of words with music and with dance. The early ballad form was characterized by an opening theme which was then repeated after each of a number of variations. Like several other popular verse forms, the ballad underwent literary adaptation, and in the process lost some of its original traits—in particular, the refrain was sometimes repeated only in part, or the end of each stanza was merely rhymed with the last word of the refrain.[2] In Italy, several of the *stil nuovo* poets whom Lorenzo greatly admired had occasionally adopted the rhythms of the *ballata,* and both the popular and literary varieties were very much alive in fifteenth-century Florence. Several members of Lorenzo's circle, notably Poliziano, made use of it, restoring to the literary *ballata* its original function as a song to be accompanied by music and dancing.[3]

The *canzone a ballo* in its presentation of an episode is in some ways "a secular counterpart to the religious *laude*, which is constructed on a like scheme and uses a refrain for a like purpose."[4] This dramatic interest inherent in the dance songs forms a basis for the more elaborate *canti carnascialeschi,* or carnival songs, whose development is generally attributed to Lorenzo himself. Florence in the fifteenth century was famous for the masques and organized revelries of its Carnival celebrations, and to these Lorenzo added a more complex dramatic framework, replacing masks with elaborate costumes and diversifying the types of song.[5]

The central theme of all the festival pieces is the celebration of love, usually joyous, occasionally with a suggestion of pain. The dance songs reflect the assumption basic to courtly poetry that love is an exalted and potentially ennobling human activity, and they form in this sense a sort of counterpart to the love poetry in Lorenzo's collection of *rime*. The phrases of the courtly lyric are common coin in the dance songs. Much of *canzone* XXI, for example, echoes famous verses from a number of stil-novistic poems: "I do not apologize for following Love, for such is the custom of every gentle heart"; "Love and honorable conduct and courtesy, to one who measures well, are a single thing." But in contrast to the love lyrics, these dance songs stress love as activity, one in which all are called to participate. The focus here is on the experience of love, not on the private emotions of the individual lover. The poet insists that love is wasted on any lady who is "proud and disdainful," and all who are not actively committed to love are told to abandon the dance. The lyrics are generally choral rather than individual in nature, and the effect is that of both a tribute to love and a rite of loving.[6]

The context of the group is frequently apparent, as in two of the more light-hearted poems, both constructed on the same conceit of the lover who loses his heart, only to find it later in the possession of the lady. In the first, the poet addresses himself to his audience and asks "Is there any lady in this company who has my heart, or knows where it may be?" (XIII), and the second is its joyful sequel: "O fair lasses, long around have I looked for my heart lost. But, O Love, I thank you most, for my heart I now have found" (XVI). While thanking Love in the refrain to each stanza for the fact that he has at last located his heart, he continues the conceit with the playful question, "Now what pain must this thief face, who did steal my heart like this?" and finally demands the just punishment for the theft:

> Bind, O Love, this thief indeed,
> burn her with the thing she stole:
> if she begs you, do not heed,
> do not look at her at all;
> let your darts and arrows fall
> till my heart revenge has found.
> But, O Love, I thank you most,
> for my heart I now have found.[7]

Some thirty-two dance songs are attributed to Lorenzo, and several others may be of his composition. Of this number, critics usually follow Carducci's lead in dividing them into three types: those celebrating the pleasures of sensual love, those mocking the love already celebrated, and those tending to obscenity.[8] But whatever its approach to the theme of loving, the particular appeal of this poetry is in its exuberance, the confidence with which it asserts the universal claims of love.

Lorenzo's major role in the development of the *canti carnascialeschi* was acknowledged in the sixteenth century by A. F. Grazzini (Il Lasca), who dedicated his collection of *Tutti i Trionfi, Carri, Canti Carnascialeschi* to Francesco de'Medici in 1559 with the statement that "this manner of celebrating was invented by the Magnificent Lorenzo."[9] The carnival songs were, in effect, a form of pageantry. The participants, no longer roaming the streets in revelry, were grouped on *carri* or carts, which were drawn through the city for the delight of the Carnival crowds. Those which staged mythological or allegorical figures were referred to as *trionfi* or triumphs, while others, in which the various trades were presented, were known simply as *carri*. As in the dance songs, the emphasis again is clearly on the group rather than on the individual. In the famous *Canzone di Bacco*, Bacchus holds center stage, along with Adriadne, but he is given a supporting cast of nymphs and satyrs, and is followed by Midas as a reminder that gold is worth nothing without pleasure. Other *canzoni* begin with the participants introducing themselves directly: "We are young gallants from Valencia, just passing through here, and already caught and bound by love for the ladies of Florence" (II). The most famous of this type is a brief choral dialogue between the two groups of "young girls" and "cicadas," or gossips, in which the girls gaily defend their pleasures against the perils of gossip, concluding with the famous verses, "Want to gossip? very well: we shall act, and you will tell" (IX).[10]

Most of these pieces do not merely present the state or activity of the speakers, but address themselves to the spectators directly, drawing them into a sense of participation. The young girls begin by introducing themselves: "We are women, as you see," and refer to their traditional enemies as "the cicadas that you see."

The sort of mime that must have accompanied these songs is readily imagined. In particular, the audience is presented with an invitation to join in the revelry, sometimes in suggestive tones, as in the plaint of the six temporarily unescorted ladies: "Woe for us, in this carnival we ladies have all six lost our husbands; and we are doing rather badly without them" (VI); and particularly, with obscene implications, when groups of young men attempt to convince the ladies of their skill as *maestri* or teachers.

The licentious tone and occasional obscene nuance of these Carnival songs have offended the critics of several centuries. Others have been startled by the use of the specific language of religious contrition to provide imagery for the cult of love: "I say 'mia colpa,' and am in great sorrow for my baseness, negligence, and every fault . . . before Love I acknowledge them all" (XXXI).[11] Yet within their context, the licentiousness and obscenity, and the freedom with which the poet adapts any imagery to his purpose, produce an effect of basic innocence. The spirit of abandon was a traditional part of Carnival celebrations. In addition, the careful study of Lorenzo's contributions to this type of poetry indicates that he was not interested in finding a mere pretext for the writing of suggestive verse. However unrestrained, the Carnival pieces celebrate love not merely as a source of physical pleasure but as an important element in human life. In both the relatively decorous and highly structured rhythms of the dance songs and the uninhibited appeals to pleasure of the *trionfi* and *carri*, it is clear that as Bowra points out, "Lorenzo is certain that it is right for men to love in this way."[12]

The naturalness and inevitability of love is stressed in a *canzone* almost as renowned as that of Bacchus, the *canzone dei sette pianeti*, the "song of the seven planets": "We are seven planets, who leave the high places in order to make the earth believe in heaven" (VIII). After declaring in unison that all human fortune is determined by their influence, the planets join in praise of beautiful Venus, who inspires all to love, and who is thus a revivifying force for the entire world. Through her influence "beasts, birds and fish know sweetness, through this the world is seen renewed." The other planets then acknowledge

Venus, the "sweet star," as their leader, presenting her to the spectators as the "kind star" who calls all to spend their days happily and not to wait in vain.

But love is not always happy. Sometimes in the dance songs the poet draws accents from Petrarch to lament the coldness of his lady, and usually to beg Love to reward his faithful service. Lacking the emotional depth and meditative tone of their Petrarchan models, these poems are frequently superficial in their effect, as in these verses addressed to Love: "Look to your honor and my desire, put an end now to my long suffering, because I am nearing my final sigh" (I). Others, however, have an authentic note in their presentation of the disappointments of love, particularly when they utilize the context of the dance itself: "Although I laugh and dance and sing, and seem so happy of face, my soul is afflicted and sad, and always in weeping and pain" (III). Even the gaiety of the celebration itself, the poet reminds us effectively, sometimes masks sadness.

While only an occasional poem tells of sadness rather than the delight of love, a single theme modifies the carefree tone through most of Lorenzo's Carnival poems. As Bowra has pointed out concerning the *Canzone di Bacco*, Lorenzo's gaiety "is achieved almost by an effort of will, by shutting his eyes to what lies before him, by flinging all his zest for pleasure into the present occasion."[13] This sense of time, with the limitations it imposes on human happiness, most often appears in the dance songs as a note of melancholy, frequently touched upon lightly, but occasionally profoundly. Melancholy deepens the poet's appreciation of beauty, with which he urges the ladies to be generous while they may: "Thus must a gentle lady have pity, and not be haughty with her beauty: because it is folly to hope always to live in youth and beauty" (II).

Occasionally, the melancholy deepens to a near tragic note which dominates an entire poem. One of the dance songs begins with the verses "Who waits for time, knows a lengthy struggle, and time does not wait, but flees away" (IX). It is almost entirely devoted to the anguish with which age looks back on lost youth. The sense of loss and pain is not merely implicit in the poem in the account of the fleeing joys of youth, for the poet adds his very personal comment: "I believe there is no greater sorrow than that caused by lost time." When he then turns in the final stanza to urge the enjoyment of the present moment, the serious tone has been so well established that the effect is one of sadness rather than joy, of constraint rather than abandon:

> Thus, gentle ladies and gaily dressed young men,
> You who have come here to sing,
> Spend your days all happily,
> For youth slowly passes by:
> I ask it in the name of that sweet fire
> Which kindles and consumes each gentle heart.

This dance song is distinguished from most of the others in that here the poet does not include himself among those who are to seize the present opportunity for pleasure; the voice belongs to someone who looks back upon the joys of youth and urges others to grasp its pleasures before it is too late. This poem bears many similarities to the *Canzone di Bacco* and the *Canzone dei sette pianeti,* which were very probably composed for the Carnival of 1490, a period in which illness was already curtailing Lorenzo's activity. Its final stanza suggests perhaps more directly than any other the real context of the *carpe diem* theme in Lorenzo's festival poetry.[14]

We thus return to the *Canzone di Bacco.* A part of its success certainly lies in the skill with which the mythological subject is adapted to the Carnival circumstances.[15] But here too, the characteristic note of melancholy modifies the abandon of the subject. After describing the delights of Bacchus and Adriadne, the gaiety of the nymphs and the little satyrs, the examples of the drunken by happy Silenus and the rich but unsatisfied Midas, the poet devotes his final two stanzas to the more general theme:

> Let all people heed me then;
> on the morrow no one feed,
> but let women and let men,
> young and old, know today's need:
> to be glad and chase, indeed,
> every sadness fast away . . .[16]

After a final shout of "Long live Bacchus, long live Love!" the poet urges the pursuit of love with an almost frenetic effect, reinforced by the rhythm of the verse and the rapid and emphatic sequence of verbs, the force in this context of the verb "burn," the final denial of weariness and pain: "Let each one play, and dance and sing! Let all hearts burn with sweetness! No exertion, and no pain!" The festival revelry thus reaches its peak, moving ever faster in an attempt to forget that it is brief. The abruptness of cold and realistic acceptance in the following verse then forms a highly dramatic contrast: "That which has to be, must be."[17] It is after this crescendo and this verse that the refrain is repeated for the final time, and its tone now is different than that of its first appearance: "Let him who wishes to, be gay: There's no certainty about tomorrow." The emphasis, originally on the invitation to pleasure and gaiety, now clearly falls on the second verse of the pair.

The *Canzone di Bacco* has been called Lorenzo's Renaissance masterpiece, and the adjective is significant.[18] Rarely does a poet succeed in capturing the spirit of his day by writing "the lyric of the century, that which sums up the aspect of the time," and in the *Canzone di Bacco* Lorenzo has done just that.[19] It is also among the most representative of his many poems, but not for its licentiousness and its famous urging of the abandonment of restraint. Only against the fleeting background of life does love, the principal subject of all the festival pieces, assume its full significance for Lorenzo. Bowra has stated that what interested Lorenzo in the cult of love was "a radiant, life-giving joy ... which transforms experience";[20] it is an affirmation of life, of vitality, and as such it is a temporary defense against the sense of inevitable loss. The *Canzone di Bacco* is representative of Lorenzo's work in its urging of present enjoyment combined with the constant sense that time brings an end to human pleasure.

Like Carnival itself, whose revelries terminate in the abstinence and austerity of the Lenten season, Lorenzo's carnival poems derive their urgent tone from the end to pleasure that is inevitably, and soon, to follow. And this end to pleasure is part of a more general failure of man's efforts to achieve a sense of permanence through whatever means. While some have seen in the *Canzone di Bacco* and other carnival songs an expression of the superficiality of the Renaissance, Kristeller points out that Ficino, too, had stressed the sadness of the rapid flight of time, and that while Lorenzo certainly conceived this "cult of the present" in a less spiritual sense, the philosopher and the poet share a point of departure, involving not only a philosophical doctrine but the very sense of life itself.[21] It is perhaps for this reason that the Carnival song is such an effective vehicle for Lorenzo's poetic effort.

II *The* Novelle

Assessments of Lorenzo's contribution to Italian letters have been based almost exclusively on his poetry. The *Epistola* to Frederic of Aragon has often been excluded because of its disputed authorship, and the *Comento* because of its philosophical orientation, while the prose of Lorenzo's letters has as yet received little attention. Recently, however, two prose texts of great interest, the short stories of *Giacoppo* and the unfinished *Ginevra*, have been added to the accepted corpus of Lorenzo's works.

Although Palmarocchi, in confirming Lorenzo's authorship, called attention to the importance of these texts, which he called "two jewels of fifteenth-century short-story writing," they have received little critical attention, either in their own right or for their contribution to the study of Lorenzo as a literary figure.[22] The problem of attribution has been a major factor in this neglect. The stories were first published in 1865. I. Del Lungo, who found them among Medici papers and published them as anonymous, recognized from the corrections and revisions in the same hand that the manuscript was the author's original. In 1923, republishing them as an appendix to his study of Lorenzo's loves, he reported their attribution "with complete certainty," and in 1931 Palmarocchi confirmed the identification through his study of autograph materials.[23] The stories are, in fact, particularly important as the only literary autographs of Lorenzo presently known.

The story of *Giacoppo* describes the marital misfortune of a Sienese citizen of that name. Giacoppo's beautiful young wife is admired by a Florentine student named Francesco, and when she welcomes his interest, the youth devises an elaborate ruse to enable them to be together. Giacoppo is led into an affair with a woman who poses as Francesco's wife; confessing his guilt to a certain Fra Antonio who is also an accomplice in the scheme, Giacoppo is told that only by direct retribution— giving back to Francesco, in kind, what he has taken from him— can he save his soul. The ruse succeeds, and at the end the young lovers' intimacy is prolonged as Giacoppo is sent to Rome to complete his penance.

The story is clearly written to entertain. Its tone is one of amused complicity between author and reader; no sympathy for the deceived husband is elicited, nor is the involvement of the priest subjected to open criticism. The indifference to conventional moral limits probably disturbed no reader of Lorenzo's day, but it has come under attack by later critics. Fatini called the work "rather obscene"; shocked by the role of the priest, he proclaimed that the mixture of sacred and profane in such a scabrous plot provoked disgust rather than laughter.[24]

Morality, however, is not Lorenzo's object of attack; at most it is an incidental victim. The story was not written as an attack or confrontation, but for amusement. If an object of derision must be identified, it is not morality as such, but rather a match, or mismatch, the author considers contrary to nature. As in a number of Boccaccio's stories, the author's sympathies are clearly with youth. The student's love for Giacoppo's wife is seen as natural: the beautiful young woman is desired by the handsome young man "as it happens to other beautiful young ladies," and the naturalness of their mutual attraction is emphasized by the parallel adjectives: "other *beautiful* ladies," "a *handsome* young man." The husband, on the other hand, is nearly forty years of age, and while he is "of a quite decent fortune," he is not an attractive mate for his young wife.

The marriage of older husband and lovely young wife as a subject of comedy is not of Lorenzo's invention. Unlike many other writers who had made use of it, however, Lorenzo offers both an explanation of his own position, and a justification. First he notes that having a beautiful wife was for Giacoppo "'among his other fortunes, or I should say misfortunes'"; while such a man may be envied as fortunate, the situation by its very nature may lead to misfortune. Cassandra finds herself married to an aging husband who is neither very handsome nor very brave, so that when Francesco expresses his love for her, it "had to follow reasonably" that she welcome his interest: "It's a very natural thing," explains Lorenzo, "having the opportunity to choose between the good and the bad, more readily to choose the good; otherwise she would have been mad enough to be locked up, had she done the opposite." Recalling the marital status of women in Lorenzo's time, one may suspect a note of irony in this defense, but as if in anticipation of such doubts Lorenzo reinforces his approval of Cassandra's choice with a general commentary:

And truly it seems to me that women have a great misfortune, and men a great advantage: for a man, however insignificant he may be, may or may not marry as he chooses; a woman, without knowing what or how, being at the disposition of others, has to take whatever is given her in order not to get something worse. . . . And so it's no wonder that errors are uncovered every day, for really one should judge them by a different standard, and give them the benefit of the doubt for the above reasons.[25]

Cleverness too is on the side of the young people. Lorenzo adds to Cassandra's good reasons for choosing "to seek another match" that she knew her husband to be "half a fool," and in the unfolding of the ruse the stolid Giacoppo does not arouse the reader's sympathy because he is foolish enough to cooperate in his own misfortune. The fact that the ruse succeeds is merely further evidence that he and his wife were mismatched; his gullibility combines with his vanity to lead him quickly into the trap set for him, and the judgment implicit in the outcome is that "it serves him right."

The scheme itself is described with an attention to detail that reveals its author's obvious amusement. Each step is carefully explained. The woman hired to pose as Francesco's wife smiles at the unsuspecting Giacoppo from her balcony each time he passes, and his vanity produces a quick response; when he begins to boast of her admiration for him, she sends him love letters, and finally notifies him that her "husband" is away. In the conduct of this affair Giacoppo becomes a doubly comic figure: not only does he find it quite natural that this supposedly newly wed young woman should find him irresistible, but the ensuing affair with her proves exhausting for one of his age and condition—a detail which, played for full comic effect, also underscores again his unsuitability for Cassandra. His exhaustion then combines with his bad conscience to set the stage for his confession.

The priest Antonio presents the idea of direct retribution, the key element in the ruse, with words cunningly chosen to conceal his knowledge of the real situation. Giacoppo must render in kind to Francesco what he has taken from him: "And you can't give it back unless you lead the woman's husband (and if she doesn't have a husband, then her nearest male relative) to be with your wife (if you have one, if not with your nearest female relative) as many times as you went to be with his wife." And here again it is Giacoppo's own gullibility, not the scandalous nature of the suggestion, which is the comic focus: he does not question the extension of the law of retaliation into the moral realm, accepting it with no suspicion that one sin might not thus be compensated by another.[26]

The author makes full use of another comic possibility: not only must Giacoppo assent to the penance stipulated by Fra Antonio; he himself must serve as go-between, persuading both Francesco and his own protesting wife to do that which they have so long desired and schemed to arrange.[27] Franco feigns shock and at first refuses; Cassandra offers even greater resistance, reproaching her husband repeatedly and finally consenting only as the one means to save his soul. As each step in his imposed penance meets with resistance, Giacoppo is led to greater efforts to achieve compliance.

In the development of its plot the story of Giacoppo points directly to a much more famous comic treatment, Machiavelli's *Mandragola*. While the most obvious comparison is that of Fra Antonio and Machiavelli's Fra Timoteo, the duped husbands also have much in common, particularly in the fact that each is led through excessive credulity to further a scheme against his own honor. Fatini compares Lorenzo's characterization of the husband unfavorably to that of Machiavelli, commenting that while Nicia in the *Mandragola* has to be persuaded to cooperate, Giacoppo in his simplemindedness exceeds the limits of verisimilitude.[28] In one sense, however, Lorenzo's Giacoppo possesses greater psychological plausibility. Machiavelli's Nicia is asked first to accept the preposterous story that the mandrake root will assure his wife's bearing a son, and then to arrange the probable death of a stranger in order to accomplish this without endangering his own health. But it is the confession of a sin actually committed that obliges Giacoppo to accept the penance imposed. The fact that his partner was only posing as Francesco's wife in no way alters the guilt of his intent. In this way, too, the author attempts to avoid moral censure for the young lovers: Giacoppo is already guilty of violating the marriage vow—which Francesco and Cassandra are preparing to violate.

The laughter in the story is also at the expense of the Sienese in general. Anti-Sienese satire, growing out of a long history of jealousy and rivalries, was a favorite subject of comedy in Florence, and in beginning by asserting that "there has always been, as many people must know, an abundance of fresh fish and fat men in Siena," Lorenzo is using references familiar within this satiric tradition.[29] Belanti, the surname of the unfortunate Giacoppo, was an old Sienese name of some importance. The possibility that Lorenzo had used the name of a real personage in his story led Del Lungo to examine records of the Belanti family, but his research revealed no Giacoppo among its members in Lorenzo's period. The question of Giacoppo's identity was later reopened by Palmarocchi,[30] but his suggestion of a Giacoppo Belanti mentioned in letters to Lorenzo from Siena is not confirmed by the manuscripts. Speculation concerning the relation between Lorenzo's story and his actual contacts with Siena remains interesting, however, because the question of Siena's shifting alliances was of major concern during many of the years of Lorenzo's responsibility for Florentine affairs. It is not coincidental that the student who cleverly makes a fool of the Sienese Giacoppo is a young Florentine.

The unfinished story of *Ginevra* is set in Pisa. Its hero Luigi, the most handsome young man in the city, falls in love with

Ginevra, the most beautiful young lady. Convention prevents him from revealing his passion directly, and prevents her from revealing any response to his interest. Experiencing all the pains of love, Luigi seeks the counsel of a more experienced friend, who recommends persistence and a number of schemes. Finally, in desperation, Luigi climbs a ladder into the bedroom of the sleeping girl. The story breaks off just as she wakes.

While *Ginevra* in its unfinished form is as long as the completed *Giacoppo*, the author's design for his story is difficult to determine. The stage at which the narrative is interrupted, the moment when the lover at last (and dishonestly) finds himself beside his love, might equally well be either near the conclusion of the story or near its beginning. The author's intent is hard to fathom because the existing portion of the story consists almost entirely of an account of Luigi's suffering. His misery may be intended as a prelude to the narration of his ensuing affair with Ginevra, or it may itself be the subject of the story, whose narrative interest would then be exhausted with the satisfaction of his passion.

Ginevra's major interest lies in its contrast to *Giacoppo*. In its introduction, so many similarities to the other story are apparent that one suspects the author of working variations on a single narrative pattern. The city that serves as background to the story is named and characterized in the first sentence, this time favorably as "an ancient and most noble city," and the families of both hero and heroine are identified, with the additional information that the hero's family still lives in Pisa. There is also the insistence that love is natural for the young, and Luigi is assured by his friend that "it's a natural thing that anyone who feels himself or herself loved, should love in return; it would be more of the nature of beasts or stones than that of humans, to do the contrary."

The positive attribution of these two stories to Lorenzo provides further evidence of the versatility that has puzzled critics. While *Giacoppo* brings to mind Machiavelli's later comedy in both conception and style, *Ginevra* reads like an exercise in Boccaccio's type of story-telling, and includes, in addition, constant references to Dante and Petrarch. In presenting the origin, growth, and suffering of love, Lorenzo not only follows these early masters, but cites Petrarch by name as his authority and includes verses from several of his poems. The writing of short stories is entirely in keeping with the interest in his literary predecessors that many of his poems also demonstrate.

While these literary influences on his stories are readily apparent, Lorenzo makes his own contribution to the genre of the *novella*. The prose of the *Giacoppo* in particular eliminates many of the elaborate constructions that had characterized Italian literary prose since the time of Boccaccio. In their place Lorenzo substituted a simpler, more flexible language that comes closer to the spoken idiom. The prose of the *Ginevra* is more derivative than that of *Giacoppo*, but both stories are presented with a freshness rare in the prose works of the period.[31] In his limited attempt at the genre, Lorenzo proved himself the equal of any short-story writer of his time.

CHAPTER 6

The Classical Influence

WHILE it is difficult to determine the exact chronology of Lorenzo's works, it is possible to discern an evolution in his major sources of inspiration, from his early poetic activity to the works of his maturity. Many indications suggest that during the later period of his life he was more and more influenced by classical sources. Of his five works on mythological subjects, it is generally assumed that two, *Ambra* and the *Selve d'Amore*, were composed after 1486, on the evidence that they are not recorded among Lorenzo's poems in Poliziano's *Nutricia* of that year. The two eclogues, *Corinto* and *Apollo e Pan*, are mentioned in the *Nutricia* and were probably composed not long before that date.[1]

Several factors may have contributed to this apparent evolution. During the last quarter of the fifteenth century a number of major classical works were increasingly studied and admired. Poliziano lectured in Florence on the *Sylvae* of the Latin poet Statius in 1480, and himself composed four Latin poems on this model between 1482 and 1486. While Poliziano was deeply involved in historical and philological studies after 1480, there are a number of correspondences between his poetry and Lorenzo's works of this period. One of Poliziano's Latin *Sylvae* is entitled *Ambra*, and celebrates Lorenzo's villa at Poggio a Caiano. This villa is also the subject of Lorenzo's own mythological poem of the same name, and passages in the *Corinto*, such as the praise of the nymph Galatea and the famed description of the fading roses, recall corresponding passages in Poliziano's poems. In a more general sense, critics have often observed that Lorenzo's style in these mythological poems is frequently very close to that of the more renowned poet.[2]

The growing popularity of the classical models and the example of contemporary poets who turned to these sources for both form and subject no doubt influenced Lorenzo, who repeatedly demonstrated his awareness of the literary trends of his time. The classical material must also have appealed, as De Robertis suggests, to his taste for literary experimentation, an interest already apparent in the variety of popular forms he used in his youthful poems.[3] Yet Lorenzo's poetic originality is perhaps most readily apparent in these mythological poems. Although they vary in quality and in range, they are not, with the exception of *Apollo e Pan*, servile imitations.

The relationship of the classical inspiration as Lorenzo interpreted it to his own sense of life and its continuity seems to be the most important factor in this evolution. In all but one of his classical poems, the mythological subject is transformed by a personal and intimate inspiration in which most of the major notes of his earlier poetry reappear in a subtler key. Through the filter of the mythological context, the poet often succeeds in reconciling the various aspects of his own complex inspiration —aspects which in the more direct and vigorous presentation of his realistic works had occasionally seemed to conflict. The mythological poems reveal a greater maturity, an increased depth of reflection on life and fortune, and a greater serenity even in the presentation of longing and pain. At their best, they are among the most successful of Lorenzo's works.

I   Corinto

The poem of *Corinto*, a brief composition of 193 verses in *terza rima*, is one of Lorenzo's two eclogues, probably composed near the end of his life.[4] In its form, its spirit, and its deliberate use of a wide variety of allusions it is perhaps the most classical of his works. While the mythological eclogue in *terzina* verse was not uncommon in the fifteenth century, the *Corinto* clearly reveals its personal inspiration, and the fusion of these two components, more successfully and consistently combined than in the *Selve* or in his other eclogue on the *Amori di Venere e Marte*, has gained it general critical acclaim.

The poem opens with a description of the night that recalls Dante in its evocation of a world at rest. Against this background

a figure is distinguished—the shepherd Corinto singing of his
love for Galatea.[5] After the opening stanzas, Corinto himself
assumes the narration, and the rest of the poem is presented in
his words and from his point of view. Corinto laments, calling
upon Nature to hear him since Galatea will not; reminding
himself of the power of verses to move the hearer, he asks the
wind to carry his plea to the nymph. This introduces the thought
that she may be hiding nearby, unwilling to acknowledge his
complaint. Thought leads to fantasy in a sequence of stanzas
in which he imagines her presence and declares how glad he
would be to serve as her companion. He then recalls an episode
in which he had seen her gaze into a fountain. Following her
there in the hope that her reflection might remain, Corinto saw
himself instead, and describes his appearance, enumerating and
illustrating his claims to strength and courage in order to prove
himself not unworthy of Galatea's attention. While he has no
hope of moving the nymph to pity, and knows that she laughs
at his weeping, he finds some comfort in the thought that her
beauty, now so cruel, is not eternal. This thought introduces
the theme of the brevity of youth, which occupies some thirty
verses and concludes with the exhortation, "Gather the rose,
o nymph, now in the fair season."

The classical derivation of Lorenzo's poem is obvious in its
eclogue form and in the name of the nymph Galatea. Extensive
studies of its sources indicate that the composite nature of
Lorenzo's poetry generally is particularly apparent in the *Corinto*.[6]
Maier demonstrates that the poem is an *opus tessallatum* combining reminiscences of many authors.[7] Primary among these
are Theocritus, Virgil, Ovid, and Aurelius, so consciously uti-
lized that some passages are near-translations.[8] In addition to
numerous derivations from the Italian vernacular tradition, too,
particularly from Dante and Petrarch, Lorenzo's own works are
frequently recalled. These include not only his other classical
poems, especially the *Selve* and the *Ambra*, but also the *Nencia*,
that other lament in a different key of a young shepherd whose
love is not returned.

It is, however, not the number of the classical sources and
allusions but the manner of their incorporation that forms the
basis of the poetic effect of *Corinto*. The classical themes receive

new life in the Tuscan setting; they are not mere literary echoes from another age, but are instead naturalized into the context of Lorenzo's own time and his own emotion. De Robertis notes that despite the classical citations and coloration, what is vital in Lorenzo's eclogue is the filtering of the classical idyll through the vernacular tradition, so that the world of Ovid and Theocritus takes on new meaning from its immersion in the reality of the vernacular.[9]

The successful poetic fusion of these various classical and vernacular influences in the *Corinto* is achieved largely through the characterization of the shepherd. The first-person presentation facilitates transitions from one key to another as the enamored Corinto's own thoughts wander. He laments and dreams, and his poem is both elegy and idyll. The rustic note is effectively introduced through his self-pitying reference to himself as *poveretto,* the diminutive of "poor fellow," and through his use of simple and direct phrases such as *te amo tanto* ("I love you so much"), the natural expression of his moments of most sincere and unguarded emotion. When he then addresses the absent nymph thinking more of her reaction than of his own pain, his words assume the tones of the *stil nuovo* with no sense of incongruity. As Maier notes, the coexistence in Corinto of rustic lover and sophisticated citizen of the fifteenth century, while perhaps occasionally disconcerting, reflects the complexity of this brief poem.[10]

Corinto, however, is not merely the embodiment of several inspirations and the spokesman for several styles. Lorenzo gives him an inner life, which, emerging more from numerous details in his speech than from the nature of his discourse, carries psychological conviction. This is apparent, for example, in his mention of the nymph's disdain for his love: "Say, don't have a heart so severe! You have already given three years of your chaste life to the hard rule of Diana: isn't this enough? Now give me a little aid, nymph, you with no pity at all" (vv. 31–35). He never returns to this theme of the nymph's vow to Diana, but when he later speaks of his skill in hunting, in stressing the qualities that deserve Galatea's attention, it is to exclaim that "with bow in hand I want to compete against Diana." The suggestion that he could best Diana at her own occupation receives no further elaboration, but the sense of competition is obviously based on his jealousy of the nymph's exclusive devotion to the goddess.

The scene in which Corinto imagines Galatea joining him is similarly revealing, and the treatment of such scenes in two other poems by Lorenzo provides a contrast that underlines the poetic effectiveness of the eclogue. When Vallera imagines himself with Nencia, his thoughts are of physical contact, phrased in terms that some critics have denounced as obscene. In *Corinto,* the imagined touch is delicate and restrained: "If I saw you here, if I touched your white hands and your lovely face, O God!" exclaims Corinto, and even his fantasy of a meeting with Galatea breaks off abruptly with a spontaneous cry which reflects his reverence for the nymph. There is no further suggestion of physical contact, although the imagined scene continues: "If you sat with me upon the grass, I would use the bark of a willow to make a pipe to play, and I would ask you to sing" (vv. 61–63). The nymph would then dance, and when she was weary, he would "gather many flowers through the meadow, and let them fall in a shower over her face" (vv. 68–69).

The falling blossoms recall the passage in the *Selve d'Amore* where Venus shows her approval of the poet's love by scattering flowers from heaven, which fall over his lady. It also provides an interesting contrast to the famous verses by Petrarch in which flowers fall over Laura as she sits by a stream (*Canzoniere,* CXXVI). Petrarch observes and describes the scene, as does Lorenzo in the later *Selve.* Corinto, however, imagines himself a participant; it is he who would gather the flowers and scatter them over the nymph, who would respond by laughing so sweetly that other flowers would spring up to take the place of those plucked in her honor. The scene is more than a lovely tableau because of the intimacy and the emotional subtlety of Corinto's fantasy.

The same primacy of personal feeling is apparent in the concluding section of the poem, where the theme of the rapid passage of youth is introduced by a description of the short life of the roses. Other poets, some classical and some more recent, had certainly used this comparison, and critics have attempted to assert Lorenzo's particular debt to the more famous verses of Poliziano on the same theme.[11] Such comparisons are inconclusive at best, however, because of the lack of a certain chronology for Lorenzo's compositions. In any case, the merit and originality of Lorenzo's treatment is not in the theme, but rather in the lyrical impulse, and in the tone of the invitation to enjoy life's delights in the full awareness of their frailty. As Maier explains, "it is a sort of pagan appeal to pleasure, shadowed by a sense of elegiac, Christian sadness which distinguishes it from the carefree *carpe diem* of Horace."[12]

Corinto continues to speak in two stanzas, in more general terms, of trees and their flowers and fruit. Some critics have considered this extension of the effective scene of the roses a weakness in Lorenzo's treatment.[13] The individual personality of Corinto justifies this elaboration, however, and adds to its validity. The shepherd describes to the absent nymph what he had observed on a recent morning: discovering a number of roses in bloom, he had turned to watch them "because," as he says, "I had never seen it before" (vv. 167–68). The careful and precise detail with which he recalls the position and degree of unfolding of each flower reflect the keen observation of one to whom this wonder was new. It is because of this newness and wonder that the total effect on Corinto is so marked: "Thus I saw them be born and die, and their loveliness pass in less than an hour"; watching the petals fall languid and pale to the ground, he concluded that "youthful flowering is a vain thing."

His surprise leads his rather simple thoughts to a type of reflection that we imagine uncommon to him: that each tree has its flower, each flower unfolds in its season, and the tiny fruit then grow until they weigh heavily on the sturdy boughs; but autumn comes, and "the sweet ripe apples" are picked, leaving the tree bare at the end of the fair season. Corinto's urgent exhortation to the nymph to enjoy the present moment is thus not a simple result of his own sense of rejection in the observation that her beauty will not last forever. The final plea is made more serious, and less personal, by the melancholy sense of the passing of all youth and loveliness. In it Lorenzo's classical inspiration and his personal tone achieve a perfect harmony.

II Apollo e Pan

Lorenzo's incomplete eclogue of *Apollo e Pan* shares with his *Corinto* the *terzina* form and the extensive use of classical sources, but with very different effect. The existing poem of 175 verses is introduced by a lengthy section describing the mount of Pindo in Thessaly, in stanzas that recall Dante's presentation of the Earthly Paradise.[14] This favored place is unaffected by the seasons and by the weather, and enjoys a state of eternal and flowering spring. Apollo, temporarily exiled from heaven after an act of vengeance, chooses to live as a shepherd in this idyllic setting. The light of his eyes cannot be diminished, but his divine appurtenances are simply replaced by their rustic equivalents: his golden bow is now of wood, as is his lyre, and instead of a crown of gems he wears one made of leaves. But as a shepherd he continues to make his heavenly music.

One day Pan chances to hear the song of this shepherd, and declares that he would like to engage him in a musical contest, were it not shameful for a god to compete with one of such lowly station. Invited to recognize the divine light in the shepherd's eyes, however, he is delighted with his worthy rival, and both sit down to begin their competition in song. As they attune their instruments, the poet interjects an invocation to his own nymph, that she recall to him the verses that were sung by the gods that day.[15]

Pan is the first to sing. In song, he tells the story of the shepherd Daphne who was struck down by Venus as revenge for resisting love. The song ends with the assertion that none can hope for pity from Cupid, and as he falls silent the beasts and even the stones are weeping. The poem is obviously incomplete, because Apollo's response, which is necessary to complete the competition, is not provided.

A poetic contest between Apollo and Pan may have been suggested to Lorenzo by Ovid (*Metamorphoses,* XI, 85–193), and echoes of Virgil and Theocritus are also abundant. As Bigi notes, the poet seems particularly intent on demonstrating his mythological erudition.[16] The classical material is occasionally colored by the freshness of Lorenzo's own conception.[17] In general, however, the poem is far less successful than the *Corinto,*

Lorenzo's other eclogue, and its limitations are readily illustrated by a comparison of the two works. The major difference is not in the number of classical derivations, but in the distance between the poet and his material; in *Apollo e Pan,* unlike *Corinto,* the classical inspiration is felt as remote by the poet himself. In *Apollo e Pan,* for example, the setting remains a mountain of legendary fame, not a place of real human habitation, and Apollo, for all his shepherd's clothes, remains a god. The *Corinto* begins with a description of a single starry evening into which the human element is carefully introduced, and which in its silent beauty serves as an effective setting for the shepherd Corinto's lament. *Apollo e Pan* opens with the verses, "There is a mountain in Thessaly called Pindo, more celebrated by the sacred bards than any other." Similarly, the song of Pan protesting the cruelty of love is based on the story of Daphne, and only artificially linked to his own experience. In *Corinto,* in contrast, the central figure is a shepherd whose idyllic setting does not conceal a very human figure; when he laments and dreams, he expresses his own pain and yearning, with all the complexity of genuine human emotion.

A number of isolated passages in *Apollo e Pan* reveal the poet's own response to the mythological story. He emphasizes the beauty of the mountain where "many colors of flowers may be seen, so lovely that one has to slow one's step, overcome by the new pleasure" (vv. 16–18); when the gods are about to begin their contest, the setting is effectively established by the suspension of all activity in hushed anticipation of the divine song: "the river Peneo stops his rapid course, the flocks forget to graze, the birds pause too, and the murmur of the leaves is stilled" (vv. 121–23). But these passages are isolated, and the poem remains cold and difficult, lacking the air of the genuine and human.

While *Corinto* can be immediately understood on its own terms, *Apollo e Pan* contains numerous references that require explanation for the reader not familiar with a wide body of mythology. Sometimes an understanding of these is essential to the larger effect, as in the reference to Pan who sits down beneath the Syringa to begin his lament about love; others are mentioned only by name, as in the reference in the final stanza to Lacaon, who wept upon hearing Pan's song and never again.[18] This procedure of enlarging the mythological context of the poem through brief references to the wider body of legend frequently dilutes and occasionally destroys its immediacy and poetic effect.

Apollo e Pan, then, while poetically inferior to Lorenzo's other eclogue, exemplifies a less original approach to the classical inspiration which forms the basis of both poems, and by this contrast serves to focus the achievement of the poet who, in the *Corinto*, made the classical world imaginatively his own.

III   *The* Amori

Among Lorenzo's several works based on classical themes, the incomplete poem of the *Amori di Venere e Marte*, with some forty stanzas in *terzina* verse, is one of the shortest and most direct. Venus, Mars, the Sun, and Vulcan speak in turn. Venus eagerly anticipates the coming of Mars, he arrives and speaks of his love, the Sun reveals and blames the lovers, and finally Vulcan laments the news of his wife's adultery. The lines are distributed among the four personages as follows: Venus, 14 stanzas, Mars, 8, Apollo, 14, and Vulcan, 4. The manuscript is incomplete following the speech by Mars and at the end of Vulcan's lament, and Lorenzo may well have projected a symmetrical presentation with fourteen stanzas allowed each of the characters.

The nature of Lorenzo's interest in this famous classical theme is at once apparent. He is not primarily concerned with the details of the situation, but rather with the attitudes of the participants, as reflected in the highly individual presentation of each. It has been pointed out that his mythological subjects are not symbols, but characters, however rudimentary, and that the poet has attempted to give a greater intimacy and humanity to the Homeric gods.[19] Venus appears as an incarnation of desire because of what her words suggest—in the crescendo of her preparation and in her long invitation to her lover—and not because of her mythological identity. Mars is the warrior almost apologetic for having proved defenseless against love, and he proclaims his emotion in terms of what he knows best, the art of war. The Sun embodies the outrage of the offended order; his role is that of an indignant moralist who speaks largely in abstractions. Vulcan is perhaps the most human of the four: where the reaction of outrage and wrath seems clearly indicated in his mythological identity, he reacts instead with grief and pain.

While the poem is called the *Amori di Venere e Marte*, it is clear from the important roles accorded all four of the personages that Lorenzo conceived of his subject in a wide sense, focusing less on the love itself than on its significance within the order it disregards. This focus is communicated primarily through the repeated contrast of secrecy and disclosure. Venus is preoccupied with secrecy in her preparations for the arrival of Mars: "Hide, Moon, the shining hemisphere: you, o dogs, do not go barking through the wood, so that the truth of the deed be not uncovered" (vv. 25–27). The Sun's reaction on discovering this concealed meeting is to deny that such secrets can long be kept. Declaring that no offender escapes being seen by "the sun, the stars, the heaven and the moon," he stresses that "every long secret has its season," so that "he who tempts fortune too much" may well encounter obstacles (vv. 73–75). After several stanzas in which he rouses all the inhabitants of his ancient world to witness the betrayal, he repeats the point, that "it is fitting that every inner secret be uncovered." Vulcan, too, when called to witness, reflects this emphasis, crying out that "I am here busy making arrows for Jove, sweating around this ancient forge, and Mars is enjoying my labor elsewhere" (vv. 115–17). But the offended husband reacts less with rage than with sadness and tenderness, while the Sun voices indignation and condemnation. It is as if the affront to which Venus invites Mars is more to the public order than to Vulcan. The goddess had asked her nymphs to take care that Vulcan not find her in adultery, "which would then be the talk of every god," and it is precisely this dreaded result which she must suffer, as the Sun pointedly reminds us: "Let no one sin, who doesn't want it talked about" (v. 81).

While the Sun is clearly the spokesman for the established order in pronouncing his emphatic condemnation, he does not speak with the poet's voice, to reveal Lorenzo's own attitude.

The Sun's judgment is unremittingly harsh; he exclaims indignantly that "it is a great injury to break the faith of marriage," and demands full punishment. Garsia has described Venus in Lorenzo's poem as "the lustful woman, who enchants already with her invitation, conscious of her power: here is the woman who deceives and induces man to deceit," and he goes on to describe her as the eternal "other woman."[20] There is of course no attempt to make Venus appear innocent, in either action or intent; she herself refers to her love as adultery and infamy. Within the poem, however, the element of calculated seduction by the Goddess of Love is somewhat tempered by her confession that she has herself been wounded by Cupid, and Lorenzo appears as interested in her feelings as in her effect on Mars and the success of her invitation.

Although he reveals obvious sympathy for the offended Vulcan, and does not condone the adultery, Lorenzo is nonetheless clearly sympathetic to the joy of love, and to the element of secrecy that heightens its pleasure. The complexity of his attitude is most apparent in one statement by the Sun who, before making the deed public, speaks directly but from afar to Venus, whose love he has just discovered: "And you, who are happy there with your Mars, you aren't thinking that Heaven is disposing of your guilt: thus often a great joy turns to woe" (vv. 70–72).

This presentation of individual passion, in which each of the three directly involved characters and the representative of the offended order are allowed to present their own positions, possesses dramatic quality, and this has been the major interest of the poem for most of the critics who have considered it. Garsia finds significant similarities to Lorenzo's one dramatic work, the play about Saints John and Paul. The political frame of reference of that play is replaced by a thoroughly classical one in the poem, but the transition from Christian to pagan conflict is an easy one, "from the spiritual conflicts . . . to those between Venus who betrays and Vulcan who is betrayed. Both are passions. In fact Lorenzo humanizes the gods of antiquity as he had humanized the heroes of Christianity."[21] De Robertis, too, makes this connection, claiming that in the distribution of roles and in the illustrative nature of the discourses, the poem represents an attempt to write a secular *rappresentazione*.[22]

Lorenzo clearly recognized the drama inherent in the mythological story he narrates, yet his presentation is not fundamentally dramatic. The four characters speak only once, in turn,
and there is no development; rather than an interplay of passions
the poet chooses a juxtaposition of passions, with a sense of the
inevitability of their conflict. The real dramatic effect is created
by the movement within each of the four individual speeches.
Venus speaks in imperatives through most of her stanzas, beginning with "Up, nymphs," and continuing with orders that
send the nymphs away on a variety of errands and create a sense
of movement and anticipation. With her invocation to the Moon
to darken the scene and to the dogs to remain silent in the
wood, there is a transition: the action, formerly ranging rapidly
and purposefully away from Venus at her command, now gives
way to languid invitation and to movement toward her.

First, she speaks to the night: "Come, happy night: and you,
deep Mani, darken the hour" (vv. 28–29), and then to her lover
himself. The word "come" is repeated in each of the final stanzas
of invitation. The first of these creates the impression that Mars
is still distant: "Mars, if the hours seem dark to you, come to
my sweet resting place, for I am waiting for you, and Vulcan is
not here to disturb our love"; while the second progresses to a
more sensual and explicit image: "Come, for I invite you naked
in my bed; do not delay, for time passes and flies. I have
covered my breast with red flowers." Finally, in the concluding
stanza of her speech, "come" occurs three times in rapid succession: "Come, Mars, come forth, come for I am alone." In
her last words, the progression from eager preparation to passionate invitation culminates with the exclusion of everything
else upon the arrival of Mars: "Let no one speak to me now
even a word." In a similar progression, Mars's references to love
become gradually more specific and sensual, until he concludes
that there is a time for love as well as for war. The Sun exclaims
over his discovery and addresses the unsuspecting Venus, then
abruptly calls all to witness the adulterous act, building through
a series of these messages to his concluding call to Vulcan, to
whom he stresses the shame of his wife's infidelity. Vulcan moves
from a general complaint about his isolation from the company
of the gods to a cry of pain that expresses his personal misfortune.

While the careful inner development of each speech accounts for most of the poem's dramatic effectiveness, another movement, from joy to sorrow, unites the individual speeches with a sense of progression. Venus's references to joy begin with her first words, when she rouses the nymphs to embellish "the glorious mount" with "songs and dances and resounding lyres." Even the obvious incorporations of mythological detail are made to contribute to the effect of happy anticipation: when she first speaks of Mars, it is to exclaim that "I have seen his happy star appear"; when Aurora is to be asked to delay the dawn, the suggestion that she "remain happy with her Titone" adds to the atmosphere of amorous delight. Mars speaks of simple physical pleasure, emphasized by its contrast to the physical exertion and hardship of the warrior's role: "It's a different matter to lie in the soft bed with one's sweet friend, and sing verses, than to weary the body with helmet and shield" (vv. 61–63). The Sun's brief contribution to this theme is also the most specific: "Thus often a great joy turns to woe." And the movement culminates in the combined sense of general injury and personal pain expressed by Vulcan.

Through the combination of these two movements, Lorenzo introduces the note of melancholy, which is his contribution to the story of the loves of Venus and Mars. Vulcan's incomplete lament illustrates the poet's success in instilling the new life of his own interest into his mythological personages. Both the expression of Vulcan's situation and that of his emotion are fresh and psychologically convincing. "It's not enough," Vulcan protests upon learning of his wife's adultery, "that heaven has cast me down to earth from the high places and deprived me of the table of the gods, and made me the blacksmith and the god of the hot fire" (vv. 109–111). When he insists that Venus must pay along with Mars for her unfaithfulness, it is with the pain of one who still loves the offender; and in his cry of pain, "Venus, my Venus, spray of the sea" (v. 118), his words, suggestive of the gentle goddess of Botticelli's canvas, form one of the more successful poetic moments in the Renaissance attempt to infuse new imaginative life into the famed mythological subjects of the classical world.

IV Ambra

Lorenzo's use of mythological material was frequently within a frame of reference provided by his own experience. One of the best examples is the poem of *Ambra*, whose title celebrates both Lorenzo's much-loved villa on his property at Poggio a Caiano, and a nymph who underwent a metamorphosis to save her from the pursuing river god, Ombrone. Lorenzo acquired the land at Poggo a Caiano in 1479, and some five years later he commissioned the famed architect Giuliano di San Gallo to construct a villa for him there. The villa was later celebrated in poems by various members of the Medici circle, notably in a work by Poliziano which was also called *Ambra*.[23] The property was surrounded by the river, and one spring a major flood caused extensive damage to the villa itself. Ovid in *Metamorphoses*, V, relates the story of the nymph Arethusa who, fleeing from the river Alpheus, is saved by the goddess Diana, and on this pattern Lorenzo constructs the tale of the nymph Ambra threatened by a Tuscan river god.[24]

The story of Ambra is introduced by a description of winter, including not only natural phenomena but also the plight of animals, birds, and human families in the harsh season. The first ten stanzas, devoted entirely to the winter setting, concentrate on the woodland.[25] First, the wood in its physical aspect is evoked, then hunters, wild beasts, and birds, but the attention of the reader is never allowed to focus on these figures and thereby lose the more general impression, which is one of austerity. The first verse of the poem refers to summer, which has fled, and the birds have fled with it. The long winter nights also deeply affect the human population: many lie awake waiting restlessly for the dawn, while lovers find the night too quick in passing. The scene changes again to the birds, this time to the cranes who fly past in formation and then rest, with one of them keeping vigil because the eagle is poised to carry off any who stray.

The introduction of the mythological element is prepared through personifications of the weather: "The summer wind fled to Cyprus, to dance there with the flowers," and the air, once serene, is troubled by harsh winds. The elements of the

Tuscan setting are specifically emphasized, as the old Mugello, a mountain to the north of Florence, "crowns its already white head with snow," and the focus gradually changes from snow to water as "irate Mugello, sometimes burdened and sometimes light, menaces the subject plain" with one or the other.[26]

This process reaches a crescendo in a description of the waters' growing force as the rivers add their own contributions. When the swollen waters reach an enclosed valley and find themselves confined, they roar in anger, frightening the shepherd who sees them from higher ground; coming out again to an open plain, they spread out wide, nearly silent, as if content. In two fine stanzas describing the terror of a family attempting to take refuge from the flood, the suggestion of force and energy is contrasted to the helpless state of the people.

This general introduction occupies twenty-two of the poem's forty-eight stanzas. Ambra is then introduced, first as the "little isle" encircled by the "haughty lover" Ombrone, the river, and we are told in a lightly veiled allusion to Lorenzo's villa that Ambra is "not less adored by Lauro, who is jealous if the rival touches and embraces her." This suggestion of the villa is immediately followed, however, by the introduction of Ambra the nymph, who goes one day to bathe in the "cold waters of Ombrone," subtly effecting the transition in presenting the cold waters not as Ombrone himself, but as "his."

As Ambra enters the waters, her presence awakens the desire of their river god, who emerges from his cave and stealthily approaches the unsuspecting nymph. As he plunges to grasp her, confident of his success, she leaps away in fright and escapes his arms, leaving strands of her hair in his hands. He pursues her without success, calling out to her to stay and join him. As he loses hope of stopping her in her flight, he sees her reach the area where his own waters join those of Arno, and he cries out to the river god Arno to block her path. With Arno's assistance, the waters surround Ambra. In her terror she calls on Diana, to whom she is dedicated, begging the goddess to preserve her chastity. She is immediately transformed into a small rocky island, but not before Ombrone arrives to witness the result of his determined pursuit.

Ovid's version of the story furnishes many of the details used by Lorenzo, although Ovid's Arethusa, after her metamorphosis, becomes a goddess of the stream into which she was transformed. On a warm day she had waded into a river, then plunged in naked, and as she swam she thought she heard "a curious kind of murmur from deep down under."[27] Fleeing naked with the river god Alpheus in pursuit, she begged Diana for help, and the goddess cloaked her in a cloud; when her pursuer remained near, in her terror the metamorphosis was completed and she became a stream. As in Lorenzo's poem, her feelings of fright are compared to those of an animal at bay.

The most notable feature of Lorenzo's version is the combination of sensuality with the emotional drama of the struggle between the god and the nymph. The element of sensuality is present from the first words describing Ambra and her contact with the waters: "when her virginal limbs entered into the dark and icy waters," the contrast itself is both suggestive and menacing, and Ombrone, emerging from his cave unseen, is naked and "burning with desire." When Ambra suddenly flees, she runs "naked and shoeless," and the few strands of hair which are left in Ombrone's hand bring about the beginning of tenderness in the god: "he curses his cruel and slow hand, when he looks at the slender fair hairs." He curses his hand because it was cruel—it had done the delicate nymph some slight harm—but also because it was slow, not having succeeded in grasping her. This ambiguous combination of the sensual and the tender, along with Ombrone's situation combining the state of a god and the pain of a lover, is reflected again in his plea that she return to him: lamenting that she loves the river's waters and not their god, he cries after her "my things are pleasing to you, but I myself do not please; and yet I am the son of Appenine, and a god." Critics have sometimes insisted that the description of Ombrone's chase is ineffective, criticizing particularly as "an artificial little game" the god's cry "O nymph, I am a river and I burn." But his dual existence—as river and as god—has been carefully prepared.[28]

From this point in the poem emotion dominates. When Arno holds back his waters to block Ambra's path, the terrified nymph is compared to a hunted animal cornered by dogs; not knowing whether to continue or to turn back, threatened on every side, she can only hope for death. The human nuance of the scene is emphasized in her plea for Diana's protection: "for I a nymph am not enough for two enemies, and both of them gods." Ombrone's grief when he arrives and observes the final stage of the metamorphosis is compared in a very effective parallel to the frustration of the dog whose prey has leaped over the wall and escaped him.

The river god is so awed by the sight that pity takes precedence over his sense of personal loss in his lament. But while he looks at the lovely growing stone that had been Ambra, the note of sensuality appears again, this time as a counterpoint to his stronger emotion of pity: "and as love and pity direct him, he bathes the stone bitterly with tears, saying 'O my Ambra, these are the waters in which it pleased you to bathe your lovely body.' " The god himself expresses his surprise that his sorrow is not now totally for himself: "I would not have believed that in such sorrow pity for myself could be overcome by pity for my beautiful Ambra, but this it is which moves me now to tears."

In the verses that follow, Ombrone becomes aware of the larger meaning of his impulse, exclaiming that while his native mountains are full of many nymphs, he had somehow chosen the most beautiful, and caused her destruction through his "cruel desire" alone. In his sorrow he cannot even invoke death, and thus finds Ambra's fate happier than his own: "In this my fate is too cruel, to be miserable, and an immortal god; for if I could at least die, the deserved and everlasting pain would come to an end." His lament for his own immortality does not lead away from the human, but rather enriches it, so that the myth permits the expression of human sadness to achieve a higher tone.[29]

The poetry of the *Ambra* has been generally admired, particularly passages such as that in which, as Brinton says, Lorenzo offers "delightful touches of his personal observation of Tuscan country life in the rough weather of winter, when 'Cold Orion with his blade menaces Phoebus if he dares to show us his fair face.' "[30] The work has been faulted, however, for its structure. Of its forty-eight stanzas, less than half treat the story of Ambra and Ombrone directly. The first half of the poem, which paints the wintry setting, has been criticized for lack of coherence, and even some admirers of the poet regret that Lorenzo attempted to combine and coordinate a variety of lyrical inspirations within "a plot which is a pretext."[31]

In fact, however, these seemingly disparate elements of the *Ambra* contribute to a single effect—the isolation of living things at the mercy of winter's harshness. It is against this background that the birds lead their families away and the cranes keep their close formation. It is the instinct of the living creature to seek close contact, as the lovers do, and for those who are isolated there is the sense of menace, as for the cranes who fear the waiting eagle. The unity of the poem lies in this struggle of living creatures against hostile forces. After this general theme is suggested, Ambra's struggle against Ombrone becomes its example, deriving much of its effect from the austerity and sense of isolation of the earlier part of the poem. One critic has suggested that the metamorphosis of the nymph gives "greater relief and savor to the elements of nature" through "an opposition which the writer had not calculated,"[32] but a reading of the poem as a whole suggests that Lorenzo's effect is very carefully and deliberately prepared. The metamorphosis itself, in which the living nymph is transformed into a small rocky island, marks the interpenetration of life and landscape that characterizes the poem from its opening verse, drawing together the various poetic fragments of the work.

V *The* Selve d'Amore

The title of the *Selve d'Amore,* or "Forest of Love," derives from the wandering of the poet's attention from one thought and emotion to another as one might wander unguided through a forest.[33] Its 174 octave stanzas are divided into the first and second *Selve,* the first (32 stanzas) containing the poet's acknowledgement of his bondage to love, the second (142 stanzas) dominated by his grief at his lady's absence. Within this very loose framework, each part consists of a series of loosely related components of varying length.

The opening stanzas of the first *selva* contain the poet's joyful praise of love, his glad acceptance of bondage. He expresses his gratitude in turn to his lady, to the lord of Love, and to

Fortune who has given him so sweet a master. An apparent digression on the destruction wrought by water, wind, and fire when each exceeds its proper measure leads to the assertion of the "benign law" which maintains a balance between all of the elements of nature, so that "a sweet chain binds them all." The poet reflects that he too was bound by a triple chain of beauty, compassion, and love on the day when he became Love's servant. Earth and heaven had combined to show their approval by contributing a setting worthy of the event: Venus scattered roses, which fell to cover the poet's lady, while Jove permitted human ears to hear celestial melodies. The lady, taking full possession of the poet's heart, transformed it from rough to gentle and concealed it within herself, where it began to sing with the poet's voice.

The second *selva* is based on the suffering occasioned by the lady's absence, immediately introduced in the opening verses: "after so many sorrows and bitter tears, those beautiful eyes still do not return." The poet now reviles time: "Oh hours now long, and you were once so short; enemies then and now to my content!" and curses his fate as he had formerly blessed it. He wishes himself transformed into a rock, a tree, or a fountain so that he might be near his lady; he goes to the place where he last saw her, and is suddenly disturbed by the thought that someone else may now be enjoying her company. As desire and jealousy combine to torment him, Hope reappears with the assurance that he will see his lady again, and that the light of love in her eyes will put an end to his tears and sighing. During Hope's lengthy description of this longed-for return, the poet's vision follows his lady's progress as she moves, honored by all, to her humble but fortunate house in which Beauty, Love, Fidelity, and other virtues dwell as her companions.

This happy scene is not to remain undisturbed, however, for in one dark corner is a pale old woman with a hundred eyes, all of them weeping, and a hundred ears. She is Jealousy, born of Chaos and nurtured on the milk of the Furies. Confined to the lower world during the Golden Age, she was later set free by the gods, themselves irritated by the effects of Love, so that she might counter his influence. This "malevolent goddess" causes such misery as she goes about the world, "turning good to ill, and always believing the worst," that the poet begs for her return to infernal exile; knowing that this prayer is vain, however, he reproaches the blind hope which had encouraged him to find false comfort.

His thoughts then turn to the past, to his first night of intimacy with his lady. This scene, a direct presentation of human love, is handled with great delicacy. The lover is not called upon to express emotions not entirely in keeping with the spiritualized reaction to the lady's presence which dominates the rest of the poem. Instead, he imagines the lady weeping, because of their separation, then allows her to present her own recollection of their past pleasure: "Here I heard his light step, and here I offered him my timid hand; here I said with trembling voice, 'Now sit down'...Here I gave myself to him completely, and here Love bound us with a knot which has never loosened." Through the restrained and modest presentation of the lady, the sensual aspects of the scene are subordinated to its complex emotional significance.[34] The imagined lament is so deeply felt that the scene becomes deceptively real to the poet. When its pleasure quickly vanishes, his pain is such that he attacks his memory along with hope itself: "O my enemy tenacious memory, which places that beautiful scene before my eyes! O my more cruel fallacious hope, that promises my heart all this and better yet!" His reproach introduces a highly original portrait of Hope as an immense woman formed and cloaked of thick mist, with a single eye which "looks ahead at high and remote things, and never turns to look behind," and two great wings to reach the heights from which fall those who follow her lead.

The poet's thoughts then turn to the Golden Age of Saturn's rule as a contrast to these torments. "Human life was longer and happier; truth was what it appeared; every desire was checked and contented, nor did the world know 'yours' and 'mine.'" All animals lived together in perfect harmony, and so did men, with love untouched by either hope or jealousy. It was Prometheus who ended this happy age: by his theft of fire from its rightful place in heaven, he created disharmony among the elements, and finally among men.

After asking Love to place him and his lady in this sweet age where their love could be eternal, the poet returns to the reality of the moment and seeks only her return. In the closing movement of the poem, after his request for a sleep that would show him his beloved, a light gradually approaches; birds herald the dawn, and flowers take on their myriad colors in the growing light. Finally the poet's lady, "his own sun," emerges from the mountain, leading Beauty and Love by the hand. He hears a melody of more than mortal sweetness, and the poem ends with the verses of this little song: "who looks upon this beauty, sighs always for sweet and eternal love."

Because the work lacks a firm narrative development, individual components have frequently been admired and anthologized with little reference to overall structure. Various sections have been praised as self-sufficient lyrics, and Capasso reflects a widespread judgment among critics when he calls the unity of the *Selve* extremely tenuous and fictitious, "forgotten completely when a page of poetry flourishes, which then develops completely independently."[35] As the title indicates, however, the poet's thoughts do not wander completely at random.[36] Dorini has suggested the fundamental importance of the Platonic concept of love in the poem, a love that is purified progressively until it is ultimately calmed in the adoration of the lady considered as the incarnation of the idea of infinite Beauty.[37] The concluding scene of the poem, and particularly the little song of the final stanza, obviously reflect the Platonic concept: "Here is true beauty, all contained in one fact; from it all the other beauties, which are dispersed in various things, take their example."

Even in the concluding scene Lorenzo carefully maintains his emphasis on the individual beauty of his lady. This emphasis is apparent in his use of personification: when the lady appears, she holds Love and Beauty by the hand, and advances between them. Her independent status is carefully maintained; she does not become an incarnation of these qualities, but dominates and controls them: "Love, who looks steadily into her two lovely eyes, redoubles the fire in which he is himself kindled, and Beauty, being reflected in that lovely face, is rendered more beautiful and more truly herself." And when the world is said to be enamored of beauty, it is not to the abstraction of Beauty but to the specific beauty of this lady that it responds.

While love is obviously the focus of Lorenzo's attention, the progressive approach to the ideal of beauty seems to concern him less than the active transformation of the self through the experience of love. It is with a tone of prophecy that Hope promises the lady's return: it will be imminent, she tells the lover, when "the light which is always glowing in your heart appears on your blind horizon, and from the peak of the sacred mountain that loving ray descends to your eyes"; the transformation of the world as nature prepares for the lady's coming will be a "new marvel," which will last "until the light of those lovely eyes appears." In the closing scene, which fulfills this prophecy, if only in a vision, the transformation of the physical world is clearly a poetic projection upon the external world of the inner experience, whose interest for Lorenzo is less in its object than in its process.

Concern with the psychology of love is manifest from the opening stanzas of the *Selve*. The poet fervently expresses his gratitude that the "sweet servitude" of Love had freed his heart from "every vile and lowly service," from "a hundred lowly cares." The effect of this moment of recognition is dramatically emphasized: when the lover's eyes, which had vainly sought their contentment in myriad objects, finally focused exclusively on the single beautiful image of the lady, "a thousand various thoughts were reduced to one alone." The lady herself, in her individuality, is secondary to this image and this function. The new focus changes the lover by providing a central image about which all of his emotional experience may be organized. Love thus appears not as a progressive ascension, in the manner of the *dolce stil*, but as a harmonizing factor.

This theme of inner harmony unifies the poetic components of the *Selve*. The moment of psychological equilibrium, experienced as ecstasy in the first *selva*, is lost to the poet in the second *selva*, and regained only through the rapture of a vision in the final scene. At the conclusion of the brief first part, the lover's heart, secure within the lady, desires only that this blessing continue "without time." The second part presents the consequences of the lady's absence: the lover is tormented by the past, the present, and even the future. His sense of personal loss underlies the depth of feeling in his praise of the vanished

Golden Age, when men loved without hope and without jealousy; in these verses the note of melancholy and nostalgia that so often touches Lorenzo's poetry is given free play in the description of a lost ideal age.[38] But the need for harmony in a more fundamental sense explains the fact that the praise of the Golden Age is not limited to its untroubled enjoyment of love. Men in that happy time, Lorenzo says, were equally tranquil in spirit, never disturbed by the desire to question beyond their capacity to understand. Desire was to the measure of nature, and men were content with what they had, untroubled by ambition.

The relation of this passage to the introductory section of the *Altercazione,* in which "Lauro" flees the cares of the city for a short time to sing the praises of the simple life, is immediately apparent. The yearning for calm and content, for inner tranquillity as well as relief from the burdens of a life of responsibility, is a recurring theme in Lorenzo's work. Here, in a famous passage, he extends his praise of a life of measure and restraint to a wider spiritual context. In the Golden Age, he declares, "wit was equal to desire, the will to the power of understanding; men were content to know of God that part which man is able to comprehend." He compares those who continually seek the causes of things which are hidden from them to Icarus, who, refusing all measure and trusting in his artificial wings, flew too high and was lost.

Lorenzo's *Selve,* then, which have frequently been harshly judged because of their "poor construction,"[39] are not a sequence of largely independent poetic fragments. They are linked thematically by the concept of harmony, apparent in many details of otherwise unrelated sections. Prometheus's theft of fire, which brought the Golden Age to an end by destroying the harmony of the elements and finally the happiness of man, recalls the imbalance of the elements described in the first *selva* to introduce the "sweet chain" of nature and the similar chain of love that contained and harmonized the poet's emotions. The destruction resulting from the imbalance of the elements is a preparation for the loss of the poet's equilibrium when the absence of his lady leaves him vulnerable to the suggestion of hope, jealousy, and his own memory.

The various sections of the two *selve* are further linked in a more general sense by the combination of an intense personal reaction to the experience of love and a more universal conception of love as equilibrium. Lorenzo succeeds in finding a mythical equivalent for personal ecstasy and personal need, in part through an imaginative use of the classical images.[40] In particular, the allegorical figures of Hope and Jealousy, which in their direct involvement in the lover's own emotions function quite differently from the traditionally drawn characters of Venus and Jove, provide an effective bridge between the personal and the mythological contexts. The concluding scene is the final successful fusion of the elements of myth and realism.[41] The rapturous vision of the return of the lady, which brings the springtime transformation of the physical world, is the fulfilment of the longing expressed in the poem, and its consummate expression. The interpenetration of the individual experience and its mythological interpretation give the work a poetic interest beyond that of its justifiably famous fragments.

CHAPTER 7

Religious and Philosophical Concerns

ALTHOUGH some critics have labelled Lorenzo's interest in philosophical questions insincere, it is a near constant in the works of his maturity. Although few of these works focus primarily on philosophical or religious questions, many reflect this concern. The *Comento*, for example, is more philosophical than literary in its orientation, and its wide-ranging discussion includes a number of philosophical topics bearing little relation to the sonnets for which the commentary is offered as explanation. Even in the direct consideration of the themes of love and beauty that predominates in the *Rime*, and in the celebration of youth and pleasure for which Lorenzo is best known, frequent notes suggest a deeper and more serious reflection on human experience: pleasure and youth are celebrated because they are of brief duration, beauty is a means by which the soul is originally moved to seek God, love is a fulfilment of the soul and the quieting of its longing.

The *Altercazione* is presented as a philosophical debate, but it is also a religious poem, in that its orientation to the question of human happiness and tranquillity is fundamentally in terms of the Neoplatonic position, which identifies the Supreme Good with God, and the search for this Supreme Good with the only source of joy for the questing human spirit. Some of Lorenzo's religious poems are largely paraphrases of earlier expressions of religious sentiment, but others reflect the inquietude of his own search. The *Sacra Rappresentazione di S. Giovanni e Paolo*, among the last of Lorenzo's works and his one venture into drama, forms an appropriate concluding chapter to his meditations on these themes, staging the victory of Christ over an emperor whose every effort has been exerted to triumph on his own terms and by his strength alone.

116

These three works, while very different in characteristics and in fundamental literary type, share as dominant traits Lorenzo's preoccupation with the search for tranquillity and his attempt to reconcile the religious beliefs that he repeatedly affirms with his own sense of spiritual anxiety. This personal note appears in the *Altercazione* in the debate about where true tranquillity may be found, in the religious poems in the note of unfulfilled longing, and in the play in the complaints of two emperors about the weariness of power. In each case, the expression of faith and promise is colored by the characteristic note of longing, of melancholy, of spiritual tranquillity sought with complete sincerity but never quite attained.

I *The* Altercazione

The interest in philosophy present in a number of Lorenzo's poems is most clearly documented in the *Altercazione,* his one work devoted entirely to the consideration of philosophical questions. In this narration of a philosophical debate some have reproached him for crossing the line that separates the writing of poetry with philosophic content from the writing of versified philosophy itself, thus producing a work which is "little more than a scholastic exercise."[1] It is clear in any case that the philosophic content of the debate is the author's real interest, and the fact that he expresses it in verse in no way modifies this impression, as a long tradition had established verse as an appropriate vehicle for the communication of philosophic opinion. The *Altercazione* rewards study with insights into some of Lorenzo's major preoccupations, and recent criticism has denied that it contains merely a paraphrase of Ficino's theories, insisting instead on its relevance for the interpretation of certain of his other works.[2] In addition, there are passages where the poetic impulse rather than the philosophic argument is dominant, so that the poem is not entirely devoid of literary interest.

The first of the six parts or *capitoli* into which the work is divided contains the "altercation" of the title. It is also the most poetic of the six, the one in which Lorenzo's own contribution is least disputed. While the section is introduced as a disagreement about "happiness according to the doctrine of

Plato," the famous philosopher is not mentioned by name, and the framework established for the debate is personal rather than doctrinal. The narrator, "Lauro," reveals at the beginning that he is visiting this country spot "to lift from my frail nature that burden which disturbs and wearies it"—a need that has caused him to leave for a time "the beautiful circle of my city's walls." He experiences the country setting as a sort of *locus amoenus*, protected from the buffeting of both weather and fortune: "I think that the air must never be stormy or dark in a place so happy and beautiful, nor can heaven or fortune do it any harm."

As he meditates gratefully on the pleasures of the place, he is recognized by Alfeo, a shepherd who is bringing his flock to water nearby. To the shepherd's question of whether he has come in order to heighten by contrast his appreciation of life in the city, Lauro replies with enthusiastic praise of the rustic life as he imagines it. More than the mere absence of vice or the presence of simple pleasures, he senses a harmony between man and nature, so that every desire is measured by nature itself. Human relations too must be happier here, he supposes— direct and open in expression, free of malice and deception: "Here you do not say one thing for another, nor is the tongue contrary to the heart"; and again, "I do not believe that it happens in such pure air that the heart sighs while the mouth is laughing, so that the wisest is the one who best conceals and varies the truth." The result, he thinks, must be freedom from care, so that sweet sleep is uninterrupted. And happy is the man, Lauro sighs, who is content with what he has. This kind of a life calls forth his highest praise: it is most conducive to human tranquillity.

The shepherd begins at once to refute Lauro's assertions. However idyllic it may appear, he says, this simple life close to nature is made unhappy by physical need and by its extreme vulnerability to Fortune, so that it is hardly a life, but rather a continuing torment. After listing some of its many hazards, he concludes that all the world may call Fortune a hard enemy. Lauro does not argue this conclusion; the end of the discussion rests on the recognition that the city dweller and the country dweller have re-enacted an old debate, and have once again illustrated the maxim that no one is ever content with his own life, each considering that of others to be more fortunate. Each must nonetheless continue with his own: "I will go where destiny invites me, you where your star calls you."

In the second chapter, Lauro and the shepherd are about to part company when they encounter Marsilio, "an inhabitant of the ancient mount," and as a friend of both disputants he is called upon to settle their altercation. He proposes to aid them by explaining what constitutes true happiness. His opening remarks eliminate both their positions from serious consideration, since it is an error to seek the good anywhere in earthly life; mortals commonly err, he explains, in trying to grasp it prematurely. There are three types of "present human good": first, that which Fortune gives and takes away; second, that which nature bestows on the body; and third, that which belongs properly to the soul. The first kind is summarily dismissed with the observation that no wise man puts his hope or trust in anything subject to cruel Fortune. The second type, "natural" or "physical," is rejected almost as quickly in the third chapter. This type includes three physical advantages: to be strong, healthy, or handsome; of these, the first two may be destroyed at any time through illness and suffering, and physical beauty, which in any case gives more pleasure to others than to its possessor, is subject to the inevitable ravages of time.[3]

Rejecting material and physical advantages in his search for the true good, which is the object of man's pursuit, Marsilio turns to his third category, the good of the spirit. Again his procedure is that of the philosopher who seeks to lead his listeners step by step to the realization of the truth. He classifies the good of the spirit as either "rational" or "'sensitive," and considers each in turn. The senses, common to both men and animals, may be a source of genuine pleasure, but they are also often a source of pain. In addition, sensual pleasure passes rapidly, leaving behind, not lasting satisfaction, but rather a sense of emptiness and bitter sadness. There remains the "rational" good, and this may be again divided, into "natural powers"—such as memory, boldness, sharpness of wit—with which we are born, and "acquired powers," which can in turn be classified as active or speculative. The definitions Marsilio offers follow well-established lines. The active power teaches men to make proper use of their natural gifts and to live in accord with the moral virtues,[4] but it is not yet our true good, which consists in turning to the realm of contemplation. Contemplation itself must have as its appropriate object, not those things that are subject to decay, but things supercelestial. If the intellect proceeds in this direction, Marsilio indicates, it is not satisfied until it discovers at last the ultimate cause, which is God.

This identification of the true good—the contemplation of God—leads to a full discussion in chapter five of the various ways in which it is possible. One may seek the experience of God either through complete cognition or through perfect love. The first, Marsilio explains, is like ambrosia for the soul, the second like nectar; and of the two, the nectar of love is sweeter. In any case, he adds, the attempt to know God through cognition alone is perilous, for it may lead to pride and thus to loss, while the way of love has its own special quality, that it may not only see, but also enjoy. With this experience of joy we reach the object of Marsilio's discourse, for the true good which man should seek is the sublime joy of oneness with God, possible only through perfect love.

The expression of this idea is strongly influenced by the imagery of Dante's *Paradiso*, but the basic conception is that of the Neoplatonists of Ficino's group. It demonstrates particularly well the attempt to combine classical and Christian views of man's ultimate objective in the search for the ultimate good. The poet makes an obvious attempt to attribute to Marsilio the best of both ancient and Christian wisdom, in presenting him as "a constant lover of the sacred Muses, nor lacking in the true wisdom, such that never does one exclude the other." Marsilio's reasoning, underlying all the various categories and antitheses of his presentation, is quite direct. It is our natural tendency to flee pain and seek pleasure, or joy. The good is naturally experienced by the soul as a source of joy. In its search, the soul is unable to find lasting satisfaction in material or physical goods, or in intermediate spiritual objects. Thus it finally turns to God, and thus discovers a good which is not transitory, partial, or disappointing. When this discovery of the supreme good is made through perfect love, the experience is that of ultimate joy.

Marsilio thus returns to the question which he had originally set out to answer, and applies this conception of happiness to the original dispute, pointing out that on these terms, neither the rustic life of the shepherd nor the city life of Lauro is to be considered best. As neither allows the attainment of the ultimate good, both are to be considered as a "sad death," and overcome. This conclusion appears entirely satisfactory to Lauro, who records that while returning to his home he was "kindled by the holy flame" to sing of the love that kindles all. His song of praise, in the form of a poetic oration, forms the work's sixth chapter.

The complexity of the work is most apparent in the relationship between the first and the following chapters. Without the first chapter, the work would be almost exclusively a systematically argued and rather detailed presentation of philosophical views attributed to Ficino. The first chapter, however, introduces the personal involvement of the poet. Although he presents himself as Lauro in the poem, Lorenzo never seriously attempts to assume a pastoral persona. One quickly recognizes Lorenzo and his own world, circumscribed by the cares of state, behind the deliberately transparent veil of classical transposition.

The veil itself is only partially effective in affording a unifying frame for the poem. Alfeo, the shepherd with whom Lauro debates, is obviously an incarnation of the classical *pastore*, but he refutes Lauro's assumptions concerning the idyllic country life in terms too self-consciously philosophical to be consistent with his assumed state. He insists, for example, that small losses and adversities are as harmful to him as major ones to the powerful city dweller, and also goes on to explain the reason for their equivalence: "The difference between wood and gold is not established by nature, as much as it is made by us, in considering one lowly, the other ornamental." And his conclusion, that all the world can call Fortune "rigid and hostile," again results from philosophic discourse of a level that does not accord well with the personage. Similarly, the introduction of Marsilio is preceded by the sound of his lyre, at which Lauro exclaims

"Perhaps the lyre which was among the fixed stars has fallen from the heavens, and the sky will be without its sign." This scene of their philosopher playing the lyre, seated on a stone beside a fountain, may have had a particular appeal for Lorenzo's small group of intimates, but it does not enhance the presentation of the ideas outside that very limited context.

More importantly, while four chapters of the six in the work are devoted to Marsilio's resolution of the question of "true happiness," that question is not really the subject of the original disagreement between Lauro and the shepherd. There is in fact no dispute at all; Lauro praises what he considers the pleasures of a calm country life, and the shepherd replies that rustic life is quite different from the idealized existence described by its admirer. But Alfeo does not insist on this basis that Lauro's life is the happier of the two, concluding rather that probably all men may complain of Fortune. The classical inspiration of the discussion is reflected in the recurrence of the idea of Fortune three times in the last four lines, in the forms of "destiny," "star," and "fate," and the generalization at the end of the chapter, that all find the lot of others happier than their own, seems the appropriate conclusion of their conversation.

But when Marsilio appears, it is a dispute which he is asked to settle, and the question is phrased in these terms: "Now since God has made us a gift of you, tell us which of us is following the true way?" At this point the contrast between the two ways of life abruptly acquires a different significance. In the original discussion, happiness and especially tranquillity were at issue, but the introduction of the "true way" presupposes some standard other than the contentment which it affords by which each way of life is to be judged; Lauro follows by asking to be told "whether our lives hold true good, or whether our destiny denies it to us, which type of life it is that it adorns, and whether the world gives it, or it is divine."

In spite of this seeming disparity between the focus of the opening chapter and that of the philosophical argument which follows, their connection provides an insight into Lorenzo's own concern with the question. The interest of the first chapter rests largely on the sincerity apparent in Lauro's reaction to the country life. His relief in leaving the city temporarily behind, his idealized conception of the harmony between man and nature, and his complaint at the duplicity of human relations in their more complex forms as observed in the city, all appear completely genuine. The main element in his own conception of the happiness of the rustic existence is tranquillity, and this is also the basis of the shepherd's refutation when he insists that country life in its own way is no more tranquil than that of the city. The implicit identification of happiness or satisfaction with tranquillity prompts the question concerning the "true way," and this in turn supplies the transition from the dispute about relative merits of two clearly illustrated ways of life to the highly abstract answer offered by Marsilio.

This theme is touched upon briefly at several points in Marsilio's exposition, particularly with the example of Mary and Martha in their contrasting reactions to Christ's presence: "Let us follow Mary," he urges, "who stayed near the holy feet, not solicitous, but quiet." Again, whatever degree of earthly perfection may be achieved, the soul, while linked with the body, is incapable of perfect understanding, and thus constantly desires to ascend to a higher level; its inability to do so is felt as the absence of tranquillity: "it remains in anxiety, and more confused within the intellect." The theme is taken up directly in the fifth chapter, where, having rejected rival claims, Marsilio finally discusses the nature of true happiness. The soul, after its long and arduous movement in search of its highest good, finally finds its object in God, "toward which the pilgrim soul moves forward, to repose in his holy residence." In this way the original dispute is resolved with a conscious return to the vocabulary of enjoyment employed in the discussion of Lauro and the shepherd: the world itself, Marsilio affirms, makes true sweetness impossible.

The oration to God that follows repeats this same preoccupation in a different key. Marsilio has stated that the soul, before being freed from the body, feels frustration and anxiety in its yearning toward something higher, and Lauro's song of praise clearly reveals these same emotions. The poet introduces the oration by stating that Marsilio's words had left him "moved to sing of the Love which kindles all," and his appeals to God repeatedly stress the fact that the need to seek God is a need

instilled in man by God himself: "Receive unto Thyself that
which Thou obligest to come to Thee, O God." This note becomes both increasingly urgent and increasingly personal, changing from abstract discussion patterned on Marsilio's answers to
a plea which gains in effectiveness by this contrast. He describes
his own thirst as too pressing, and the rather formalized sequence
of praise alternating with prayer gives way to questioning:

> O abundant grace, o pious mind,
> how can it be that each least thing
> should be fed and fulfilled by Thee,
> and man, Thy marvellous creation,
> who reveres and adores Thy holy name,
> should be left with such an ardent thirst?

The passage concludes on a note in which doubt cannot be excluded: "man is more miserable than a dumb beast, if Thou
dost not make him happy in Thy land."

In the following verses Lorenzo draws back from the direction
taken by this lament, stating that he hopes for an end to his
torment from God's abundant grace, and affirming his belief that
God does not deceive man in his mortal suffering. Even the highly
traditional conclusion returns, however, to the antithesis of
calm and anxiety, with one of its simpler and more effective
statements in the image of the true *patria* or homeland: "Where
the homeland is, there is true repose; where there are father and
homeland together, the son finds rest; there is the supreme
good, true, and abundant." The soul, which would find its peace
only in God, must seek refuge from the coldness, diffidence and
desperation which struggle within it. The final stanza summarizes
the oration, declaring that in loving God's infinite beauty one is
freed from the anxiety which torments the heart.

It is the sense of personal need for this tranquillity which
unifies the otherwise disparate elements of the opening discussion, Marsilio's detailed exposition, and the concluding prayer.
It is clear in the opening chapter that Lauro does not consider
his countryside a true *locus amoenus,* although he describes it
in such terms.[5] The opening stanza serves to provide a psychological frame of reference for his reaction to the scene: "Drawn

on and escorted by sweeter thought, I had fled the harsh civil storm to bring my soul to a more tranquil harbor." In answer to Marsilio's surprise at finding him far from his responsibilities, he replies that he had come away from civic cares so that his soul might re-create through contemplation the pastoral life he envies. The intense need within Lauro for a place such as the one he describes is most effectively communicated. This need explains one of the major discrepancies between Ficino's own presentation in his *De Felicitate* of the search for the supreme good and that in Lorenzo's poem, where the philosopher's assertion of the Epicurean ideal of tranquillity is replaced by the example of Mary and Martha and the poet's choice of the contemplative over the active life: "Let us follow Mary."[6] In passages such as these the poetry acquires a tone of particular seriousness and intensity, and the anxiety which the verses reveal has the conviction of lived experience.[7]

This personal need underlies the unique effect of the closing oration. Buck, who observes that metaphysics in Lorenzo's work takes the form of metaphysical longing as well as of pure speculation, asserts that in the *Altercazione* the question is primarily that of finding a solution to the problem of happiness, and that this was the only major speculative question Lorenzo seriously treated.[8] It is clear in any case that Lorenzo's treatment of the question is not dispassionate; nor does the final oration have the detached, philosophical tones of Marsilio's explanation. While Lauro accepts the solution proposed by Marsilio, it has not been experienced in the poet's life, and he greatly desires it; in this respect the oration clearly is related to Lorenzo's religious poem which begins "O God, O Supreme Good, how may it be that I seek Thee alone and never find Thee?" The emphasis is on the psychological aspect of the religious question: not on the ultimate salvation of the soul at the successful conclusion of the quest, but on the relation of the anxious, questing soul to that which promises satisfaction of its need. While the great resemblance of the oration to Ficino's prose *Oratorio ad Deum theologica* has been pointed out, this emphasis is peculiarly Lorenzo's own.[9]

Much critical attention has been directed to determining the date and circumstances of composition of the *Altercazione,* and such investigation is particularly tempting because of the obvious reflections of the poet's own group and situation in the poem. We know that Lorenzo had composed a part of the famous concluding oration late in 1473, but the evidence for the dating of the other parts remains inconclusive.[10] Some critics question whether the work was originally conceived as a whole. Martelli suggests, for example, that Lorenzo originally composed a more modest work in three chapters, which he worked on early in 1474, then incorporated into the longer structure near the end of his life. He argues plausibly that the initial section containing the debate and the first of the encounter with Marsilio formed part of the original work in three chapters, as did the concluding verses of the fifth chapter, and that the entire central section was a later addition based on Ficino's work.[11] The extreme variation in the quality of the verse, as well as the difficulty in perceiving a unity in the work as a whole, would then be explained by the author's never having given a final form to the additions which fill out the longer version.

Further speculation has been occasioned by the work's close relationship to the two other well-known texts, Ficino's *De Felicitate* ("On Happiness") and Cristoforo Landino's *Disputationes Camaldulenses*. Landino's work is in dialogue form, and its participants, "Alberti," "Ficino," and "Lorenzo," discuss many of the questions raised in the *Altercazione,* beginning with a debate on the comparative merits of the active and the contemplative life and progressing to a discussion of ways of attaining the Supreme Good, or God. Ficino's work is addressed in letter form to Lorenzo, and presents the philosopher's own views of the Supreme Good. The connection between these works and Lorenzo's poem is further suggested by Ficino's remarks which open his letter to Lorenzo, in which he relates his letter to a discussion which had taken place at Lorenzo's villa at Careggi. Scholars disagree about the precise relationship of these three texts; some suggest that Ficino's letter is based on the *Altercazione,* others that the *Altercazione* derives from the letter, and still others that one or both of these texts are influenced by Landino.[12] Wadsworth, in a detailed study of the three texts, concludes that Ficino's *De Felicitate* was written "as an answer to and refutation of the second book of the *Disputationes.*"[13] He assumes that Landino's work had been the subject of the discussion at Careggi to which Ficino refers, and that Lorenzo, not satisfied with Landino's presentation of the question of the Supreme Good, wrote his own version, adding the opening discussion and the concluding prayer.[14]

While the derivative nature of most of the material in the *Altercazione* is easily demonstrated, the poem is not without interest for the study of Lorenzo's work. It offers proof that Lorenzo's involvement with the Neoplatonic philosophy expounded by Ficino was more than superficial. And precisely because of its derivations, it provides a clear illustration of Lorenzo's tendency to assimilate his wide-ranging sources and dominate them in a literary work bearing his own stamp. Even in the long passages in which Lorenzo translates Ficino's Latin original, Martelli's detailed comparison demonstrates that while many verses seem mere sketches, full of the flaws of quick and unretouched translation, others reveal a genuine talent through which "Ficino's prose, more graceful than vigorous, finds in the Italian translation an unexpected dramatic quality and an exceptional synthetic power."[15] With regard to the philosophical content, Wadsworth is surely correct to observe that the *Altercazione* "is more than a school exercise, Lorenzo more than a docile pupil."[16]

II *The Religious Poems*

Lorenzo's religious poems form one pole of his often-cited "dual inspiration." While the carnival songs urge the full enjoyment of the present moment, and most of the other works reflect an obvious delight in the things of this earth, these poems focus on more serious subjects. Whether openly religious in theme or reflecting their author's meditations on the passing of time and on death, they introduce a different perspective within Lorenzo's consideration of human activity.

The religious poems may be considered in three categories: seven *capitoli religiosi* (brief compositions in *terza rima*), a few sonnets, and nine *laudi* (songs of praise). The group of the *capitoli* is the earliest, probably dating, along with the oration which concludes the *Altercazione*, from before the Pazzi conspiracy of 1478. At least some of the sonnets of religious inspiration may be placed after that date, and the *laudi* were almost certainly composed near the end of Lorenzo's life.[17]

The *capitoli* consist of five orations and two later poems of a more personal inspiration.[18] The orations were at one time cited as evidence of Lorenzo's own religious concerns during an early and relatively untroubled period of his life. But in this particular case, investigation of the complex problem of Lorenzo's sources led to a completely different conclusion, establishing that all five poems were renderings into Italian of works well known to Lorenzo and his circle: the first from Boethius's *Consolation of Philosophy*, three from specific Hermetic texts, and a fifth from Psalm 1.[19] Their faithfulness to their originals explains the occasional heaviness of their style, including a number of latinisms included in an obvious attempt to retain the exact phrasing of the texts. They are not translations, however, but paraphrases, and contain additions which elaborate the thought of the text or attempt to clarify it. These additions add little to the effectiveness of the originals, and sometimes detract from it; as Rochon points out, they neither enrich the thought nor give it a more poetic expression.[20]

Because the intent of these paraphrases is clearly to provide accurate versions, their poetry may be considered primarily as a skillful exercise in verse translation. Their contribution to the study of Lorenzo's works is important, however, in the choice of the texts, which clearly reflects an active interest in the Neoplatonic teaching of Marsilio Ficino. The *Consolation of Philosophy*, one of the most widely read works from its composition in the ninth century until Lorenzo's own time, has its roots in the Platonic tradition, and with the legend of its author's Christian martyrdom it offered philosophers an unusual opportunity for attempting the combination of Christian and Platonic elements. More specifically, the particular section of Boethius's work which Lorenzo chose to render into Italian was itself based on the first part of Plato's *Timaeus*.[21]

The choice of Hermetic texts is even more directly related to Ficino's interests. These works, probably composed in third-century Alexandria under the influence of Platonic philosophy, were long thought to be written by the ancient Hermes Trismegistus, and thus to antedate all of known Western philosophy. The fifteenth-century humanists, finding in these venerable texts an apparent confirmation of many of their own views, studied them with the greatest interest. Ficino's name was closely associated with their propagation: in 1471, two years after the first edition of the group of Hermetic texts known as the *Asclepsius* appeared, he published a Latin translation of the first fourteen sections of the Corpus Hermeticum under the title of *Pimander*.[22]

The two remaining *capitoli* are original. Both are longer than the paraphrased poems, and both present as their basic theme the error of placing too great a value on earthly things. The contexts of the two poems are very different, however. One of them, probably the earlier, is addressed by the poet to a friend who is mourning the death of his young daughter, while in the other the poet addresses his own "lazy wit," rebuking and exhorting it on the basis of his own regretted errors.

The verses addressed to the bereaved friend, Gianfrancesco Ventura, present an unusual variation on the poem of consolation. After expressing his shared sorrow, Lorenzo quickly urges the father to control his grief, and offers to relieve his suffering through reasoning about the nature of death. While he assumes that the soul of the young girl has passed to a blessed state in heaven, and thus claims that grief is for one's own loss alone, Lorenzo does not stress her greater happiness as consolation. His major contention is that while the father may feel her death to be the more cruel because of her youth, she was in fact fortunate in dying at a pure and innocent age, when salvation is more easily attained; the longer one remains on earth, he asserts, the more one loses of innocence, thereby "adding fuel to the eternal fire."

Lorenzo is thus led to his real lament, which is not for the dead, but for the living, and not merely for the bereaved father but for the human state. The poem had opened with the announcement that his own amorous style and sweet song, which once were happy, had turned to weeping, with the recognition that its former happiness had been due only to his "blind desire." The suffering of his friend is then added to that of the poet, and the double sorrow affords the pretext for a general treatment of the need to detach oneself from earthly affections.

The poet himself, in terms of his own former love, had been led to acknowledge the passing of time and the disillusionment with earthly attachments which it brings, and within the context of his shared sorrow, he exhorts the father to derive from his mourning the wisdom "not to love a mortal thing so deeply." Never in this insistence on the transitory nature of human life is the father urged to focus his thoughts on his daughter in her now blessed state, and from this to gain inspiration for the better conduct of his own life. This counsel to the bereaved, usual in poems of the type, is replaced in Lorenzo's poem by words of near reproach: "But why did you place so much affection in a mortal thing, fragile and short-lived, as if its pleasure were to be eternal?" The poem's weakness is that its declared subject, the consolation offered Ventura, functions as a simple pretext for the expression of this more general theme. Lorenzo's grief for his lost amorous illusions and the father's grief for his dead child, while both illustrating the limitations of human attachments, are too different in type, and do not combine to form a genuine context for the poet's lament.

The second of these poems, which begins "Awake, lazy wit," is more successful in the presentation of this theme. As in the poem for Gianfrancesco Ventura, direct address is employed in a lament for the human state and an exhortation to transcend it. But here the poet addresses himself and his own wit, and his expressions of regret thus have a more direct and authentic note. The false goals of honor, utility and pleasure pursued in his youth have all distracted him from the true path, and in warning his wit to free itself quickly, he points to the general weakness of human nature: "our fragile craft" is subject to the conflicting forces of hope, fear, joy, and sorrow, and so is easily lost. This in turn leads to another warning, to break with past habits and seek the eternal before it is too late. The poem shares some of the defects of that addressed to Ventura: the personal note alternates, sometimes abruptly, with the abstract, and the tone is frequently more discursive than genuinely poetic. The poet's dependence on Petrarch and especially on Dante is apparent in almost every line. Yet the result is frequently expressive and moving, and occasionally the verse rises to the resonance of its Dantean model: "You have consumed the verdant springtime of your life," he cries to his soul, "and perhaps the rest will be the same, until it be the last evening of winter."

Among Lorenzo's poems collected under the title of *Rime* are a few that deal with religious themes. As he follows his master Petrarch in the composition of the love poems that compose this group, Lorenzo follows him also in the different yet closely related vein of the lover's eventual lament that he has given so much of himself to love. Closely connected, as in Petrarch, with the theme of the passing of time and of youth, this lament reflects a sense of disillusionment, a recognition that earthly love has failed to satisfy and fulfill his longing. But as this only rarely leads in Lorenzo's poems to considerations of spiritual alternatives, these few works are more appropriately considered with the collection of the *Rime*.

Three sonnets clearly belong to the religious type. Sonnet LIV is the most direct of the three and the least poetic, being in fact a question on a point of doctrine. The opening stanza presents the image familiar from Dante, and especially from Petrarch, of the soul's flight into a tranquil harbor from a tempestuous sea, followed by a question concerning grace: given that all things proceed from God, and given also that divine grace operates only in that which is already well disposed to receive it, the poet asks whether grace or good inclination is primary. There is no attempt to conceal the doctrinal nature of the sonnet, and the closing verse is specific: "Now you reply to the doubt which has been raised."[23]

Two sonnets to Ginevra de'Benci should also be included among the religious poems. Both are addressed directly to her, and both are apparently written to praise her recent decision to enter monastic life. The first, "Follow that fervor, devout soul," encourages this "new citizen of Bethany" in her dedication, and counters possible difficulties, particularly those arising from the harsh and jealous reactions of others. In its calm and reflective tone, the poem manages to convey genuine respect for the cloistered life and its object. The second poem to Ginevra, however, lacks this unity of tone and of feeling. Its basic theme sounds a warning to the lady not to look back, but to express it the poet resorts to a bewildering variety of examples. The opening stanza presents the story of Lot's wife transformed into a pillar of salt for having turned to view the burning of her wicked city, and the next stanza urges the nun, newly escaped from her own city "which burns continually in every vice," not to turn again to the world she has left behind. But this dramatic parallel of the two women fleeing, with its implicit warning to Ginevra, is followed by the disconsonant image of the fleeing girl as the lost lamb which the good shepherd bears back to safety in his arms, and finally by the account of Orpheus who, by looking back, lost Eurydice. The combination of examples from Old and New Testaments and from mythology is not in itself unusual, particularly since Christian meaning was frequently sought in the stories of Orpheus and other legendary figures. But in Lorenzo's poem these sources remain distinct and sharply different in tone and reference. The sonnet, which relies heavily on tradition and rhetoric for its effect, is far less successful than the poem to Ginevra which treats a subject within the poet's personal range of comprehension—the attempt to turn away from the world while faced with the disparaging comments of others.

The songs of praise, the *laudi*, like the earlier orations, are derivative, but in a very different sense. In contrast to the studied renderings of Hermetic and Neoplatonic texts, these are literary versions of essentially popular poetry. The popular *laudi* had developed from the combination of music with vernacular verses of praise in the thirteenth and fourteenth centuries, and had then been adapted as a literary form. Many of these poems parallel well-known profane ballads, using the same metric systems, and their manuscripts frequently indicate the ballad-melodies to which they were to be sung. While the poets composing *laudi* attempted to retain the original impression of religious fervor, these efforts to give literary expression to the popular form are not frequently successful.[24]

Lorenzo does not convey deep feeling about two of the major themes from which the authentic popular *laudi* derive: the figure of the Virgin and that of the crucified Christ. The most famous of his songs of praise, that which seems closest to the popular strain in its ballad-like repetition of the refrain "may everyone praise Thee, Mary," is highly traditional; as Garsia indicates, it is "full of grace, but devoid of passion."[25] The poem in which

Christ himself speaks from the cross, inviting sinners to witness and approach His broken body, is frequently strained, and the poet's efforts to express the horror of the scene seem labored. Similarly, the verses in which Lorenzo reproaches his own hardened heart with the view of the crucified Christ, while somewhat more intimate, appear primarily as an exercise in this type of poetry, as is the case even with the more famous poem beginning "Jesus, since I have tasted your sweetness . . ."

While these *laudi* on traditional themes seem to lack personal inspiration, two poems in this group communicate deep sentiment. The hymn of joy beginning "Sinners, arise, one and all, let us rejoice with desire" strikes a very authentic note, and makes effective use of antithesis, the major poetic device in most of these songs of praise. While its theme is the resurrection of Christ, its basic inspiration is in the miraculous offer of hope to sinners, who may share in the celebration of the holy event. The exultation is effectively portrayed through the simple and direct celebration of the day itself: "This is the day that God has made"; "Oh blessed and worthy night, your Maker loves you well!" Its emphasis is neither doctrinal nor intellectual, but rather an intuitive grasp of the joyful significance of the resurrection, accessible to all, and communicated through that sense of the cycles of the human experience to which Lorenzo was so responsive.

The most effective poem of the group is that beginning "Oh God, oh Supreme Good, how may it be that I seek Thee alone and never find Thee." It focuses again on the personal relationship of the imperfect soul to God and to the mystery of salvation. In contrast to a number of other poems, it is tightly and carefully structured. Each stanza until the final one elaborates some aspect of the search introduced in the opening verses, and each concludes with the word "never" or one of its compound forms.

There is a definite movement in this poem that is psychologically valid and acute. From the original statement of the theme, a confession of a very personal kind, the poet's repetition of his failure in four consecutive stanzas is followed by a sudden address to his searching soul: "Now! sad soul, why are you still seeking for the blessed life amid such cares and pain?" He then urges it to turn away from the distractions of the world to search in a different way, and the following four stanzas assume that this search will be rewarded, an affirmation of confidence emphasized by the repeated use of the future tense: "Then will the eye see invisible light"; "the soul will run quickly . . ." This movement concludes in the penultimate stanza with the exclamation, "Oh holy water, if I reach Thy font, I will drink, and thirst no more forever." But in this last statement we are reminded that the fulfillment of longing described in the previous stanzas has not yet been attained, and the word "if" draws us abruptly back to the present state, one of a search as yet unrewarded, to introduce most effectively the intimate appeal of the final stanza. No longer addressed to God, the Supreme Good, but to Jesus, it concludes with the urgency of the request, "heal Thou this wound of Thy making." While the poet never questions the belief that God is indeed to be found, nor that the search is worth any sacrifice, the tone of the poem is still tentative, conveying the hesitancy of someone who describes with yearning and humility the ultimate satisfaction of finding God, but from the intensely personal perspective of one who has not yet found Him. More than a song of praise, it is a plea and a lament.

The differences between the *laudi* are so great that it is difficult to recognize the same author's hand in all of these poems. While those based on traditional themes—the hardened heart confronted with the sacrifice of Christ, the praise of the Virgin, the words of Christ on the cross—contain effective and moving verses, they do not fully succeed as *laudi* because they are basically imitative and rhetorical, with no spontaneous impulse animating their expressions of praise. It has been suggested that Lorenzo was not capable of genuine religious poetry because he himself lacked an intimate experience of religious passion.[26] It is true that most of his religious verses are on traditional themes and presented in a traditional manner, with the paraphrased poems representing the extreme example of this tendency. But in addition, he occasionally created a poem in which his own religious sentiment, firmly founded in the experience of this world rather than in a mystical sense of the divine, was freely expressed. Whether in the form of *capitoli,* sonnets, or *laudi,* these verses are the best of his religious poems. And while his religious poems never rise to a level comparable to his finest achievement in other types of poetry, they are frequently effective as expressions of the individual soul in its faltering search for spiritual meaning.

III *The* Sacra Rappresentazione di San Giovanni e Paolo

Lorenzo's single venture into drama, the "sacred play" about Saints John and Paul, presents few of the major critical problems of his other works. There is little dispute about the period of its composition, its sources have been documented, and its tone and fundamental intent are unambiguous. Nonetheless, it is not an easy work to assess, and its complexity is reflected in the wide range of critical appraisals. It is interesting mainly as an example of how Lorenzo imposes the stamp of his own originality on traditional forms and materials. Because it was composed during the last years of Lorenzo's life and deals with questions of particular interest for him, the play also provides a rare, intimate insight into its author.

The development of the dramatic type known as the *sacra rappresentazione* is closely associated with Florence in the fifteenth century. Here as in other parts of Europe, representations of the lives of saints and of sacred legend, originating in liturgical scenes, were among the earliest evidence of vernacular drama. But in Florence from an early date, a second dramatic tradition was evolving, a largely mimetic tradition centering on the celebration of the city's patron, Saint John. The emphasis in these little festival pieces was on spectacle and technical virtuosity. Their fame spread throughout Italy, and they were imitated in many other towns; for the Florentines, they were a source of intense and competitive civic pride.[27] Dramatic representation of the lives of the saints was then adopted by the composers of works for the Florentine festivals, and the result was the mixed form known as the *sacra rappresentazione.*

Since the works known by this name are extremely varied, only a very general definition is possible. In its entire range, the *sacra rappresentazione* has been called "a dramatic composition which proposes to show the punishment of vice and the reward of virtue."[28] In this orientation, as in its subjects, the *sacra rappresentazione* clearly reveals its liturgical origins. But it is a flexible form, unified only by the subject, so that as many times, places, and characters as are required to illustrate the exemplariness of the saint are permissible. A place is now found on the stage for personages from all walks of life, whose activities are not always edifying; most often these reveal, through their disguises of legend and scripture, the life of contemporary Italy.[29] While the subject remains religious, the focus of interest is altered to such an extent that comedy in some instances becomes the dominant note. As Kennard points out, "in the majority of *sacre rappresentazioni,* where the personages of the play are drawn from daily life,—robbers, rogues and peasants, kings and clerics ... the comic contends with the grave, and the laughter of the audience is provoked by many means."[30]

The Medici, prominent in the evolution of all the arts in Florence, were also interested in the *feste* or public celebrations, that part of the cultural life of the city in which the populace was most directly involved. Lorenzo in particular showed a great interest in them, to the point of drawing Savonarola's direct accusation that "he occupies the populace with spectacles and celebrations, so that it will think of itself, and not of him." But whatever his motives, Lorenzo is credited with recognizing that the celebrations had degenerated into a chaotic form of revelry in which little of value remained, and with attempting in a semiofficial manner to restore some of their former dignity and civic significance. It is probably due only to direct Medici influence that poets of standing, notably Feo Belcari, contributed to these essentially popular productions, and that the type was thus elevated, at least in a few works, to the level of dramatic literature.[31]

While Lorenzo's role as patron was thus of primary importance in revitalizing this type of dramatic presentation, his personal contribution as poet was even more far-reaching. Some scholars have suggested that his play was composed for the celebration of the marriage of his daughter Maddalena to Francheschetto Cibo, son of Innocent VIII; others have suggested that it was presented by the boys enrolled in the Compagnia del Vangelista in 1489, with Lorenzo himself participating. There is evidence, however, that his involvement was occasioned by a specific request for a piece to be performed by the Company of the Evangelist in February 1491.[32] It was accompanied by music by the Flemish composer Arrigo Isaac, one of Lorenzo's favorite musicians who had held both important official positions in the musical life of the city and the private post of instructor to Lorenzo's children. By all accounts, the production of the work was a great success, and the text was printed several times in the following years.[33] The mere fact of Lorenzo's having written a *sacra rappresentazione* raised the status of these plays and accorded them considerable prestige, and the popularity they enjoyed later in the century may be attributed largely to his contribution. The several attempts of Feo Belcari, his only predecessor of note in attempting the type, had been brief and sketchy, and it remained for Lorenzo to provide a fully literary example.

In Lorenzo's play, Saint Agnes, recently martyred, appears in a vision to her sorrowing parents. Constance, daughter of the Emperor Constantine, is miraculously cured of leprosy when she turns to the saint, and as a result, she is converted to Christianity and takes a vow of chastity. Gallicanus, the head of Constantine's army, is sent to defend the Roman Empire in Thrace, but asks for Constance in marriage as his promised reward. The girl herself counsels her father to consent, but on the condition that Gallicanus leave his two daughters with her and take with him her two Christian officers, John and Paul. Gallicanus suffers a defeat in battle, but John and Paul persuade him that a vow to God will assure victory. He then sees a young man bearing a cross, who tells him to take his sword and follow; he is led to the enemy camp and there slays the king, whose army surrenders. Thus Gallicanus returns triumphant, but having taken a vow of continence, he frees Constance from the promise of marriage and goes away alone to dedicate himself to God. In the meantime his daughters have been converted by the example of Constance. Constantine abdicates in favor of his son Constantino, but the new emperor, and his two brothers after him, lose the imperial title and their lives. They are followed by their cousin Julian, who determines to rule the crumbling Empire with a firm hand. He denounces the Christians, and persecutes and finally condemns John and Paul. After the death of these martyrs, the Virgin heeds the prayer of Saint Basil and sends Saint Mercury to strike down the apostate emperor, who dies acknowledging the victory of Christ.

One of the editors of the play stresses its "occasional" nature, urging us not to expect too much of a piece destined above all to "amuse the Florentine spectators of average and slight culture, reinforcing with smiling participation and without excessive literary scruples their traditional tastes and preferences."[34] Because Lorenzo sought to adhere as closely as possible to the fundamentally popular form of the *sacra rappresentazione* in his treatment of his material, the play has frequently been dismissed as mediocre. There is no division into acts, no serious attempt at *vraisemblance*, complete disregard of chronology and of the dramatic unities. Some have dismissed Lorenzo's aim and his achievement as the production of an "instructive spectacle," a sort of "history in dialogue" of the establishment of Christianity.[35]

The play's fundamentally dramatic conception is nonetheless clear from a comparison with its source. Despite the predominantly popular nature of most of the plays of this type, and the fact that Lorenzo's own central characters are celebrated widely in medieval legend, he turned to written sources for his material, relying primarily on the written accounts of the lives of the saints. The collection known as the *Legenda aurea*, or "Golden Legend," had a prominent place in the Medici library, and Chiari has argued that the part of that work written by Jacopo da Voragine was Lorenzo's "true and single" source, demonstrating that it contains the material on which all of the eight episodes of Lorenzo's version are based.[36] The major changes Lorenzo makes in Jacopo's account all serve to heighten the dramatic effect. Constantine, rather than retaining imperial power until his death, abdicates in favor of his son, focusing attention on the transfer of power and providing a context for his long discourse advising his heirs about its proper use. The persecution of the martyrs occurs before the audience and is not merely recounted by a witness, and the Virgin is accorded a role. More important, it is the Apostate Emperor Julian himself, not his messenger as in Jacopo's narrative, who is stricken at the end of the play, making possible the highly dramatic conclusion in which he acknowledges the victory of Christ.

The play possesses a fundamental unity, although this is not to be found in observance of the formal dramatic unities. It appears rather in the psychology of character, and in this sense Lorenzo's choice of subject for his one attempt at the drama is highly significant. While the play receives its title from the names of the early Christians martyred at its conclusion, Saints John and Paul, its real protagonists are the two emperors, Constantine and Julian the Apostate. The saints, spokesmen for Christianity, play their assigned role, but remain more spokesmen than genuine characters; in much of the play their dramatic function is primarily that of confidants.[37] Both emperors, however, play psychologically complex roles: they hesitate, doubt, and suffer. It is through them, too, that we perceive the real focus of the play's interest: the possession of power, its use, and its consequences.

In the typical *sacra rappresentazione* as summarized by Kennard, the focus is entirely on the saint: "Scene follows scene, from birth, through a life of suffering and final martyrdom for the Faith, to the entry of the holy person into eternal bliss."[38] In Lorenzo's play the "holy persons" themselves are relegated essentially to the background of the drama, making way for a diversity of points of view which itself sets this play apart from the others of its type.[39] It distinguishes Lorenzo's work too from both its source in the legend and from the well-known earlier work on the same subject by the German nun Roswitha. Chiari points out that while Jacopo da Voragine was primarily interested in the miraculous aspect of the events and Roswitha in the conversions, Lorenzo is concerned with the theme of the hunger for power and its inexorable insatisfaction.[40]

The character of the aging Emperor Constantine is so convincingly drawn that he has generally been accepted as Lorenzo's spokesman. Several of his pronouncements on political life, not essential to the play's central subject, have been considered direct allusions to the state of Florence and the Medici position in the city. The abdication scene of the old emperor reads like a treatise on the proper use of power, and some have taken it to be Lorenzo's own political testament, while others have suggested that the author was using the words of his personage, not to counsel his sons, but to justify himself and his own authority.[41]

In the expression of the responsibilities of the ruler, one note is persistent: that of the weariness and anxiety which accompany power. Constantine repeatedly stresses this: "Know this, that ruling is nothing but care, weariness of both body and mind; nor, as it appears from the outside, is ruling sweet." This stress reappears in the words of Julian when he explains that the power of the ruler derives from the ruled and must constantly be applied in their interest. Some of these notes have an intensely personal ring, as when Constantine says that "often he who calls Constantine happy is much better off than I, and does not tell the truth," and when Julian asserts that because of the ruler's heavy and constant obligation to his subjects "one cannot say that he is a private person." These comments are of particular interest because the play was written in the years immediately preceding its author's death, perhaps as late as 1491, and thus offers the reflections of a mature and experienced Lorenzo. Chiari may well be correct in suggesting that what we find in the play is not Lorenzo's political testament, but his private one.[42]

The emphasis is basically secular, and thus does not contribute directly to the aims of a *sacra rappresentazione*. Some critics, admiring Lorenzo's treatment of this theme and the intense humanity of the principal characters, maintain that his dramatic effectiveness gives way abruptly to the commonplace and declamatory when the religious element is introduced—when, for example, Gallicanus and his daughters are converted, and when Julian proclaims his defeat at the end of the play. For this reason, some have maintained that the religious factor is merely the framework within which Lorenzo makes clear his real interest, the interplay of human passions independently of any spiritual preoccupation, and that this framework, while remaining formal and external to the play's real interest, forces him to "pretend to have faith in all those things which do not move him at all but which are nonetheless supposed to be the essential part of the drama, allowing it to keep the label of 'religious.'" The ending in particular has been criticized as hardly natural, reserving as it does an exemplary punishment for a man whom the author so clearly admires.[43] But this very element, the defeat of a man otherwise so strong, lends most of the religious as well as the dramatic force to the play's conclusion.

It is in this context that one must study the major role accorded Julian in the play. While the sympathetic portrayal of Constantine is to be expected, Lorenzo's treatment of Julian is more unusual in a work whose aim is to celebrate Christianity. Far from appearing in an unsympathetic light, the great Apostate takes his place along with Constantine as a *porte-parole* for Lorenzo. He dominates the stage, a man of action and of courage, and in his determination to be victorious lies the key to Lorenzo's reconciliation of such a character with the Christian direction of his theme. Before Julian enters the scene, the word "victory" has been sounded again and again in the play, sometimes with ardent desire, sometimes with irony, sometimes with religious fervor. When Constantine hears that Gallicanus, returning victorious, desires to marry his daughter, he cries out "and thus having triumphed is vexatious to me, if victory brings this with it." Later, on learning of the conversion of this same soldier, he comments that "he who conquers the world and subdues the devil, is the certain heir of true victory."

These two themes of power, that of weariness and that of the determination to be victorious, culminate finally in Julian and his struggle, in which the claims of worldly power and action are pitted deliberately against the claims of Christ. Julian's is a near-obsessive preoccupation with ascendancy, which he defends with all the considerable means at his command. Loria describes him as "a Roman, hard, haughty, fully conscious of being the supreme ruler, on earth, of a disintegrating world for whose safety and duration he intends to fight to the bitter end."[44] When Julian goes so far as to assert that "the king and the wise men are above the stars," Lorenzo's use of the ruler for his own Christian theme becomes apparent. The Apostate's last words, spoken at the time of his death, are not a straightforward acknowledgment of Christianity. Their force derives rather from the character of the man who utters them: "Deceiving life! o our vain efforts! already my spirit leaves my breast. O Christ of Galilee, you have won after all!" Julian sees

Christianity's triumph in the triumph of Christ himself, and phrases it as a victory of one man over the other, ending a long struggle for domination. Much more than the standard theme of the exaltation of the martyrs, such a confrontation of wills appeals to Lorenzo, and the fact that such a man as Julian acknowledges his personal defeat by Christ is clearly, in the author's eyes, a very strong statement of the force of that religion which Christ represents.

The resulting *sacra rappresentazione* has far more depth and complexity, in both content and execution, than any other example of this dramatic type. While it is true that Lorenzo's characterization is generally more effective in presenting secular rather than religious passion, the religious interest here is in some respects deeper than that of the typical *sacra rappresentazione* which focuses, according to a pattern, on the death of the martyrs. The recurrent note of weariness with worldly affairs, combined with the transposition of the idea of victory from the earthly to the spiritual plane, produces the genuinely religious effect of the play by pointing up the insufficiency of this world to meet man's deepest needs. These elements are not abruptly identified, but carefully developed throughout the play: "and only faith conquers the world: therefore this faith appears the true victory, which has eternal glory as its prize." There are few lines in all of Lorenzo's literary production more revealing of their author than Julian's final cry; in expressing even the religious theme in terms of power and victory, few works are more indicative of the way in which Lorenzo's own forceful personality both informed and seconded his literary effort.

Conclusion

IT is probably still true, as Rochon commented in 1963, that the moment has not yet arrived when one can attempt a comprehensive view of Lorenzo's life and work. The polemic about his life continues, and still occasionally extends into the study of his literary activity. A growing number of careful historical studies, however, by making the man himself appear less an enigma and by enlarging our knowledge of the specific Florentine context of his activity, have made it less difficult to approach the poetry itself. Recent editions of Lorenzo's work, along with some important studies of the difficult problems of attribution and chronology, have laid the foundations for a new assessment of his literary work.[1] It is now a relatively easy task to refute claims that Lorenzo as a writer was insincere, a dilettante, or primarily politically motivated; a close study of his work convinces the reader that his poetic activity was both serious and sustained. That activity, which emerges as a major contribution to Italian letters, is so varied and complex that even after detailed consideration it cannot be readily summarized.

Lorenzo's most obvious contribution to the Italian literary tradition rests on his defense of the vernacular as a literary language. While he generally reflects the ideal of the humanists, and especially their aspiration to recover the heritage of the Greeks and Romans and to build on that glorious past an equally glorious present, the fact that he composed all of his own literary works in the vernacular marks a highly significant departure from the literary emphasis of his period. The impact of his specific defense, of his patronage of vernacular writers, and of the prestige he accorded to the *volgare* through his own compositions do not, of course, admit of precise measurement, but they occurred at a moment when the primacy and even suitability of the vernacular for literary use were being questioned.

They constituted an important contribution in determining the future direction of Italian letters.

Variety is the most apparent characteristic of Lorenzo's literary work. While it has often been the object of criticism as an indication of poetic dilettantism, of lack of genuine interest in content, or of a superficial concern with literary values, it is in fact an indication of the opposite, of the seriousness of Lorenzo's poetic activity. His activity in all areas is characterized by a note of restlessness, the desire to experience life to the fullest, the dissatisfaction with facile definitions and solutions whether political, personal, or philosophical. This restlessness suggests that he was not content to explore the limits of his literary talent in traditional love poetry alone. It must be remembered that if Lorenzo's choice of poetic forms was wide-ranging, so was his experience; if his work is to be characterized as experimentation, it must be in terms of that serious attempt to use literary form as a means of capturing and shaping experience.

The restlessness that explains the variety of literary modes also explains the much-discussed range of attitudes in his work—from the uninhibited celebration of pleasure to earnest reflection on the Platonic interpretation of beauty and love, and finally to the most intimate aspirations of the soul in search of God. There is remarkable variety in this range of tone and attitude, but far less contradiction than has frequently been asserted. While the Renaissance reaffirmation of the pleasures of this world is widely recognized, the prevalent Neoplatonic philosophy elaborated its theory of the soul's search for God in terms of the search for joy and fulfillment; the tension between this world and the other was one which philosophers as well as poets were attempting to resolve.[2] Lorenzo, man of action as well as poet, was near the center of that tension, and his work is its honest and direct expression.[3] Several students of the period have commented on its serious debate about the comparative merits of the active and the contemplative life, and this question is repeatedly reflected in Lorenzo's poems, not only in the open discussion of the *Altercazione* but also in the apparently opposite poles of his festival and religious works.[4] Life and youth and pleasure are celebrated within a context of fleeting earthly joy; it is the ever present sense of their impermanence and limitation which causes the poet to turn to philosophical speculation about the nature of human happiness, and finally to address himself directly to God. And in neither the frenzied celebration of pleasure nor the more meditative works does he completely silence the restlessness that strikes a constant note in his poetry.

His work has sometimes been dismissed as a mere series of exercises in the prevalent literary modes of his day. The parts of his work most admired by his contemporaries—the use of poetic forms and themes well established in the vernacular tradition, the imitation of the most celebrated literary models, the inclusion of Neoplatonic debate—do not offer the most interest for the modern reader. Works such as the *Rime* and especially the *Comento,* upon which his poetic reputation was largely based in his own time, frequently appear cold, distant, and difficult of access today.

While the element of derivation cannot be minimized, in his best works it is neither sterile nor merely imitative. Lorenzo was a poet-reader *par excellence,* gifted with an extraordinary ability to assimilate his sources; his education and his own interests made him familiar with the best of both the classical and the vernacular traditions, and his ability to make his wide range of sources the vehicle for his own personal inspiration characterizes his best poetry.[5] For almost every one of his works, one or more literary sources may be readily identified. Yet in his best work the derived material is transformed: the primitive hunting poem became the *Uccellagione,* the comic country pieces suggest the *Nencia da Barberino* whose literary achievement is best illustrated by the inferior works of imitation that followed it. The classical themes, so often subjected to facile imitation in Renaissance poetry, acquire new life in their fresh Tuscan context and provide a responsive medium for the expression of Lorenzo's own sentiment. The genre of the *sacra rappresentazione* receives in his single play its first genuinely literary expression.

From his own time on, Lorenzo's fame as statesman has overshadowed his activity as a poet, and his literary work has seldom received the detailed consideration accorded the compositions of Pulci and Poliziano. Yet in his demonstration that traditional literary forms, both classical and popular, could be adapted to the fresh content and attitudes of his own complex new age, Lorenzo contributed, perhaps more than any other poet of his time, to the renewal of Italian poetry.

Notes and References

Preface

1. Francesco Guicciardini, *The History of Florence*, trans. C. Grayson (New York, 1964), p. 10.
2. D. De Robertis, "L'esperienza poetica del Quattrocento," in *Storia della letteratura italiana*, III (Milan, 1966), p. 460.

Chapter One

1. H. Baron, *The Crisis of the Early Italian Renaissance* (rev. ed.; Princeton, N. J., 1966), p. xxvi.
2. See Baron's discussion of "Florence and her Cultural Mission," *ibid.*, pp. 414–17.
3. See P. Monnier, *Le Quattrocento: essai sur l'histoire littéraire du XVe siècle italien* (Paris, 1901), p. 53. For a detailed study of the sources and importance of this interpretation of the city's history, see D. Weinstein, "The Myth of Florence," in N. Rubenstein, ed., *Florentine Studies: Politics and Society in Renaissance Florence* (London, 1968), pp. 15–44.
4. See K. Hillebrand, "La politique dans le mystère du XVe siècle: Lorenzo de Médicis," in *Etudes historiques et littéraires* (Paris, 1868), p. 208.
5. For an account of the early Medici rule, see S. Brinton, *The Golden Age of the Medici* (London, 1931). L. Martines discusses the Florentine attitudes toward the humanist in detail in *The Social World of the Florentine Humanists, 1390–1460* (Princeton, N. J., 1963), pp. 238–62.
6. For Lucrezia's interests and her influence on Lorenzo, see A. Rochon, *La jeunesse de Laurent de Médicis* (Paris, 1963), which describes her as "pious without narrowness of mind and without prudery" (p. 23).
7. For Lorenzo's education, see the detailed study by Rochon, *La jeunesse*, especially pp. 30–46, "A l'école des humanistes."
8. For an assessment of these charges, see E. Bizzari, *Il Magnifico Lorenzo* (Milan, 1950), p. 40, and Rochon, *La jeunesse*, pp. 93–97.
9. See E. L. S. Horsburgh, *Lorenzo the Magnificent and Florence*

in her Golden Age (London, 1908), pp. 133–35; the translation from Lorenzo's *Ricordi* is Horsburgh's.

10. Y. Maguire, *The Private Life of Lorenzo the Magnificent* (London, 1936), pp. 135–36.

11. See the study by N. Martelli of "I pensieri architettonici del Magnifico" in *Commentari*, 17 (1966), 107–11.

12. See S. Barfucci, *Lorenzo de'Medici e la società artistica del suo tempo* (Florence, 1945) for a comprehensive study of Lorenzo's wide-ranging patronage of the arts.

13. Rochon, *La jeunesse*, p. 328.

14. See Horsburgh, *Lorenzo the Magnificent*, pp. 135–37.

15. C. Ady, "The Quincentenary of Lorenzo de'Medici," *Italian Studies*, 5 (1950), 64; and Guicciardini, *History of Florence*, p. 8.

16. For a summary of critical views of Lorenzo's politics, see B. Maier's study in *I classici italiani nella storia della critica*, I (Florence, 1959), pp. 329–48, and particularly A. Palmarocchi, *La politica italiana di Lorenzo de'Medici* (Florence, 1933).

17. Bizzari, *Il Magnifico Lorenzo*, p. 299.

18. "Ficino's doctrine turned the humanists away from a political action for which the tyrant wished to assume alone the responsibility and the glory. The men of letters ceased to be citizens conscious of their duties to become courtisans anxious to please the master" (Rochon, *La jeunesse*, p. 329).

19. F. Bérence maintains that without a generous impulse, a real knowledge of art, and a deep attachment to the things of the intellect Lorenzo and the other Medici patrons would not have been able to single out the most gifted men in several areas; *Laurent le magnifique ou la quête de la perfection* (Paris, 1949), p. 244.

20. P. O. Kristeller, *Studies in Renaissance Thought*, II (New York, 1965), p. 90. For a discussion of the fame of the Florentine Academy, see the chapter on "The Platonic Academy of Florence," pp. 89–101.

21. N. Machiavelli, *Istorie fiorentine*, bk. VIII, in *Opere*, ed. E. Raimondi (Milan, 1966), p. 78.

22. Brinton, *Golden Age*, p. 193.

23. For Savonarola's indictment and the "romantic thesis" of Lorenzo as tyrant, see B. Maier, *I classici italiani*, p. 335, n. 2.

24. F. De Sanctis, "Storia della letteratura italiana," in *Opere*, ed. N. Gallo (Milan, n.d.), p. 356; and F. Ravelli, *Attraverso il Quattrocento: la poesia popolareggiante* (Turin, 1904), p. 11.

25. For this judgment and others in the same key, see B. Maier, *I classici italiani*, p. 334.

26. E. M. Fusco, *La lirica*, I (Milan, 1950), p. 174.

27. See A. Rochon, "A l'ombre du laurier," in *Florence au temps de Laurent le Magnifique* (Paris, 1965), p. 188.

28. G. Previtera, *La poesia giocosa e l'umorismo,* I (Milan, 1953), p. 278.

29. See, for example, Rochon, "A l'ombre du laurier," p. 188; and B. Maier, *I classici italiani,* p. 341.

30. S. Della Palma, "Prologo alla sacra rappresentazione del Magnifico," *Aevum,* 36 (1962), 431, n. 2.

31. B. Cicognani, *La poesia di Lorenzo de Medici* (Florence, 1950), p. 363.

32. P. Pancrazi, *Nel giardino di Candido* (Florence, 1950), p. 44.

Chapter Two

1. "And perhaps there will again be written in this language things which are subtle and important, and worth being read," Lorenzo states in his "Comento ad alcuni sonetti." Unless otherwise noted, all quotations and translations of Lorenzo's works are based on *Scritti scelti di Lorenzo de'Medici,* ed. E. Bigi (Turin, 1965).

2. P. O. Kristeller, *Studies in Renaissance Thought,* II, p. 120.

3. *Ibid.,* p. 131. For a detailed account of the *questione della lingua,* see B. Migliorini, "La questione della lingua" in *Questioni e correnti di storia letteraria,* ed. A. Momigliano (Milan, 1949), pp. 1–75; and also H. Baron, *The Crisis of the Early Italian Renaissance,* chaps. 13–15 (pp. 273–353); the discussion by D. De Robertis, "L'esperienza poetica del Quattrocento," in *Storia della Letteratura Italiana,* III, pp. 358 ff; C. Grayson, "Lorenzo, Machiavelli, and the Italian Language," in *Italian Renaissance Studies: A Tribute to the late Cecilia M. Ady* (London, 1960), pp. 410–32.

4. De Robertis, "L'esperienza," p. 358; B. Croce, *La letteratura italiana,* ed. M. Sansone, I (Bari, 1967), p. 189.

5. Baron, *The Crisis,* p. 538, n. 31.

6. Rochon concludes that from his fourteenth year Lorenzo had such a solid knowledge of Latin that his admirers wrote to him frequently in that language, and he notes the letters in Latin which Lorenzo would himself write to Ficino at the age of twenty-five (A. Rochon, *La jeunesse de Laurent de Médicis,* p. 34).

7. Baron, *The Crisis,* p. 333.

8. *Ibid.,* p. 336.

9. The defense of the *volgare* appears at the beginning of the third book of Alberti's *Della famiglia.*

10. R. Cardini, who publishes the text of the address, attempts to fix the date of the Oration on Petrarch, favoring 1467 instead of the more generally accepted 1460: "Cristoforo Landino e l'umanesimo

volgare," *Rassegna della letteratura italiana*, 72 (1968), 267–96; see also M. Santoro, "Cristoforo Landino e il volgare," *Giornale storico della letteratura italiana*, 131 (1954), 501–47.

11. Baron, *The Crisis*, p. 352.

12. For these influences on Lorenzo during his youth and early manhood, see Rochon, *La jeunesse*.

13. See De Robertis, "L'esperienza," pp. 462, 463.

14. *Ibid.*, p. 488.

15. The date of 1476, proposed by B. M. Scanferla in "Per la data della Raccolta Aragonese," *Rassegna bibliografica della letteratura italiana*, 21 (1913), 244–50, is generally accepted; see also L. W. Ferguson, "The Date of the *Raccolta Aragonese*," *Modern Philology*, 23 (1925), 43–45.

16. Three texts are assumed to reproduce the original *Raccolta*, but some of the poems are slightly altered, and there has been some disagreement concerning the reconstruction of the text. M. Barbi in *Studi sul Canzoniere di Dante* (Florence, 1915; reprinted 1965) devotes a chapter to the *Raccolta* and studies the derivative manuscripts and their relationship. For the contents of the *Raccolta*, see I. Maier, *Ange Politien: la formation d'un poète humaniste (1469–1480)*, (Geneva, 1966), pp. 226–27, n. 37.

17. *Opere di Lorenzo de'Medici*, ed. A. Simioni (Bari, 1914), II, p. 353.

18. See E. Bigi's discussion in "Genesi di un concetto storiografico: 'Dolce Stil Novo,' " *Giornale storico della letteratura italiana*, 132 (1955), 339.

19. References to the *Epistola* are to the edition by Simioni in *Opere*, I, pp. 3–8.

20. See especially G. Stange, *Lorenzo il Magnifico* (Bremen, 1940), p. 201, nn. 7, 9, for the sources of references from Petrarch in the *Epistola*.

21. Especially I. Maier, *Ange Politien*, pp. 230–31.

22. For the competition, see A. Altamura, *Il certame coronario* (Naples, 1952); see also V. Rossi in *Il Quattrocento (Storia letteraria d'Italia)*, V (3rd ed., Milan, 1945), p. 115.

23. For examples of this theme, see P. Monnier, *Le Quattrocento*, II, p. 53.

24. For a bibliography of Ficino's use of the *stil nuovo* concepts, see E. Bigi, "Lorenzo lirico," in *Dal Petrarca al Leopardi, studi di stilistica storica* (Milan-Naples, 1954), p. 43, n. 23. The preference for Cavalcanti in the *Epistola* is discussed by Rossi, *Il Quattrocento*, pp. 345–46, and by Bigi in "Genesi," pp. 340–41.

25. Bigi, "Lorenzo lirico," pp. 23–25, and "Genesi," p. 339.

For a general interpretation of Lorenzo's position with regard to the *stil nuovo* tradition, see A. Lipari, *The Dolce Stil Novo according to Lorenzo de'Medici* (New Haven, 1936), and Chapter 4 of this volume.

26. Bigi, "Lorenzo lirico," p. 24.

27. References to the *Comento* are to Bigi's edition in the *Scritti scelti*, pp. 297–449.

28. Lipari, *Dolce Stil Novo*, p. 50, n. 4.

29. See *Scritti scelti*, ed. Bigi, p. 306, n. 2, in agreement with the conclusions of M. Santoro in "Poliziano o il Magnifico?" *Giornale italiano di filologia*, 1 (1948), 139–49. F. Palermo in *I Manoscritti palatini in Firenze ordinati ed esposti* (Florence, 1853), I, pp. 664–65, noted the similarity of the descriptions of the *volgare* in the two works, but his observations have been generally discounted.

30. See the observations of De Robertis, "L'esperienza," p. 372.

31. For a more detailed discussion, see Sara Sturm, "The Case for Lorenzo's Authorship of the *Epistola a Federico d'Aragona*," *Renaissance and Reformation*, 8 (1971), 69–78.

Chapter Three

1. The title *Caccia col Falcone* was that given the work by Roscoe, who first published it in 1795. It exists in six manuscripts: in two it has no title, in a third "Lorenzo de'Medici al compare," and in the remaining three either "Uccellagione" or "Uccellagione di starne." For a discussion of the manuscripts, see A. Rochon, *La jeunesse de Laurent de Médicis*, pp. 436–37; and M. Martelli, "La tradizione manoscritta dell *Uccellagione di starne*," *Rinascimento*, 5 (1965), 51–85.

2. Rochon, using letters and other documents, favors the end of the summer of either 1472 or 1474 (*La jeunesse*, pp. 438–39); Bigi gives some weight also to arguments favoring its composition during Lorenzo's very early youth (*Scritti scelti*, pp. 153–54). Martelli presents the evidence of the manuscript tradition that the poem narrates "not the events of a single hunt, but of one among the many" ("La tradizione," p. 62).

3. Rochon, *La jeunesse*, p. 438.

4. M. Bontempelli, *Il Poliziano e il Magnifico, lirici del '400* (Florence, 1910), p. 261.

5. Rochon summarizes the poems of this type as consisting of a variable number of verses of unequal length with the position of the rhyme or assonance also varying, and the only fixed element in a closing pair of hendecasyllabic verses (*La jeunesse*, p. 440).

6. Rochon discusses briefly other theories about the origin of the form and their relevance to Lorenzo's work. D. De Robertis, discussing the influence of Pulci's realism also, concludes that recalling precedents is of no value here, since the various elements are combined within a wider range of representation ("L'esperienza poetica del Quattrocento," in *Storia della letteratura italiana,* III, p. 492).

7. Rochon, *La jeunesse,* p. 441.

8. Cited by Bontempelli, *Il Poliziano,* p. 261.

9. Rochon, *La jeunesse,* p. 447.

10. *Scritti scelti,* ed. Bigi, p. 15.

11. Rochon, *La jeunesse,* p. 455.

12. A. Capasso, *Tre saggi sulla poesia italiana del Rinascimento* (Genoa, 1939), p. 127.

13. *Scritti scelti,* ed. Bigi, p. 15.

14. As Rochon points out, the position that each occupies for the procession is indicated with a minuteness that almost suggests protocol (*La jeunesse,* p. 446).

15. *Ibid.,* p. 458.

16. Capasso, *Tre saggi,* p. 125.

17. *Ibid.,* p. 127.

18. Martelli, "La tradizione," p. 76.

19. Rochon outlines some of the structural symmetries: in the first two strophes, which present the coming of day, the various elements in the second octave are arranged in an order that is the reverse of the first, so that the two strophes together form a rigorously composed tableau; the literary arrangement is of such concern that each of the three friends is the hero of two sections (*La jeunesse,* p. 454).

20. The important recent edition of the *Simposio* by M. Martelli (Florence, 1966) suggests a number of changes from former editions.

21. Rochon, *La jeunesse,* p. 549.

22. The new dating is proposed by Martelli in his edition; see pp. 3–27 for his discussion of chronology, and the review by E. Pasquini in *Giornale storico della letteratura italiana,* 144 (1967), 117–18, for a discussion of the problems raised.

23. Valori's *Laurentii Medicei Vita* was written in 1494, two years after Lorenzo's death; it was reworked between 1517 and 1521, with a dedication to Lorenzo's son, then Pope Leo X.

24. Rochon, *La jeunesse,* pp. 546–47.

25. *Simposio,* ed. Martelli, p. 20. Martelli also offers as evidence Poliziano's *Nutricia* of 1486 in which the *Simposio* is mentioned along with other works which Lorenzo was probably composing during that period. This evidence has been disputed by Pasquini in his review, which suggests that the coincidence of testimony is

due to Valori's having used the *Nutricia*'s verses in his own account (*Giornale storico*, p. 119).

26. Pasquini writes in his review of Martelli's book that the improvements seem obvious after the fact, and are sufficient to radically improve the entire presentation (*ibid.*, p. 116).

27. The quotation is from A. Garsia, *Il Magnifico e la Rinascita* (Florence, 1923), p. 185. Carducci is cited in Bontempelli, *Il Poliziano*, p. 273.

28. For a discussion of this view, see Rochon, *La jeunesse*, p. 570.

29. U. Dorini, *Lorenzo dei Medici detto il Magnifico* (Florence, 1949), p. 286.

30. E. L. S. Horsburgh, *Lorenzo the Magnificent and Florence in her Golden Age* (London, 1908), p. 425.

31. For a discussion of these works in imitation of Dante and Petrarch, see Rochon, *La jeunesse*, pp. 550–53.

32. De Robertis, "L'esperienza," p. 490.

33. Cited in Bontempelli, *Il Poliziano*, p. 272.

34. Rochon notes that Lorenzo may be demonstrating more intelligent respect for the works he seems to be mocking than that of those who copied them without art or reason (*La jeunesse*, p. 564).

35. See Rochon's discussion for examples of allusions to Ficino's work and to Lorenzo's own poems (*ibid.*, pp. 560–64).

36. Horsburgh, *Lorenzo*, p. 462.

37. Pasquini, in *Giornale storico*, p. 116.

38. The words are Horsburgh's: "What freakish twist in him gave rise to *I Beoni* it is difficult to divine. . . . It thus equally pours ridicule on things in their nature contradictory and opposed—on drinking, and on Dante. Yet Lorenzo was a genuine student, and a declared lover of Dante. . . . *I Beoni* therefore as a psychological product is curious and baffling, more interesting perhaps as a problem than as a work of literary art" (*Lorenzo*, p. 424).

39. Dorini, *Lorenzo*, p. 283.

40. V. Rossi, *Il Quattrocento, Storia letteraria d'Italia*, V, p. 345.

41. Bontempelli calls it "uniform and monotonous" in *Il Poliziano*, p. 272, and Previtera describes most of the poem as "a long and oppressive enumeration, of figures which are too similar" (*La poesia giocosa e l'umorismo*, p. 277).

42. Previtera points out that Lorenzo's obvious purpose was to "laugh and to divert the *brigata* which gathered at his court with the caricature of the most famous drunkards, known to all" (*ibid.*, p. 275).

43. De Robertis, "L'esperienza," p. 490.

44. For a summary and discussion of the three versions, see M.

Fubini, "I tre testi della 'Nencia da Barberino' e la questione della paternità del poemetto," in *Studi sulla letteratura del Rinascimento* (Florence, 1947); for a discussion of the ensuing controversy, see Rochon's chapter on "*La Nencia da Barberino*: une longue polémique" (*La jeunesse*, pp. 358–99).

45. Fubini, "I tre testi," p. 94.

46. Fubini supposes that the fact the poem lent itself to the recital of single octaves or of groups of octaves led eventually to the destruction of the equilibrium of the original and the accentuation of the elements of caricature and jest at the expense of the poetry (*ibid.*, p. 96).

47. See, for example, Rossi, *Il Quattrocento*, p. 338, for the "improvisor" theory.

48. P. Toschi, "Paternità naturale e paternità spirituale della *Nencia da Barberino*," in *Studi di letteratura popolare* (Florence, 1957), p. 129.

49. For Marchetti's arguments, see "Bernardo Giambullari, autore della *Nencia da Barberino*" in *Nuova Antologia* (1949), 406–12, and "Stato civile e lineamenti della *Nencia da Barberino*" in *Aevum*, 25 (1951), 415–34.

50. F. Ravelli points out that in the same dialect a familiar form of the masculine name Lorenzo is "Nencio" (*Attraverso il Quattrocento, la poesia popolareggiante* [Turin, 1904]), p. 93. Bontempelli identifies "Nenciozza" as "a popular pet name for Nencia which is a shortened form of Lorenzo's name" (*Il Poliziano*, p. 250, n. 8). Toschi, "Paternità naturale," p. 129; see also *Opere*, ed. Simioni, pp. 360–61; and *Scritti scelti*, ed. Bigi, pp. 127–28.

51. De Robertis, "L'esperienza," p. 493.

52. This ballad, recorded in the notebook of Giovanni Scarlatti, is presented by D. De Robertis in "Un nuovo ritmo nenciale in un manoscritto fiorentino della prima età di Lorenzo," *Studi di filologia italiana*, 21 (1963), 201–15.

53. Fusco, *La lirica*, p. 179.

54. Rochon's opinion is that such details were introduced by Lorenzo to make it clearly understood that his poem was not to be taken too seriously (*La jeunesse*, p. 434, n. 144).

55. *Ibid.*, n. 148.

56. L. Di San Giusto, *La vita e l'opera di Lorenzo il Magnifico* (Florence, 1927), p. 146.

57. Fusco, *La lirica*, p. 179.

58. See, for example, Rochon, *La jeunesse*, p. 406.

59. Rochon points out that the demands of his daily work have accustomed Vallera to express himself in concrete terms, which thus

come to him naturally when he speaks of Nencia and of his own suffering (*ibid.*, p. 413). Of the notes of sensuality in the poem, Fubini observes that they are different from similar types in the *Beca da Dicomano* and other works within the Nencia group, because here they serve to complete the presentation of the character, while those of Lorenzo's imitators are an end in themselves, included merely to provoke easy laughter ("I tre testi," p. 93).

60. It is "an artistic means to confer on the evocation of the life, the character, and the sentiments of an enamored peasant a truth which it would hardly have attained if Vallera had used a language other than that which he spoke every day" (Rochon, *La jeunesse*, p. 413).

61. See, for example, *ibid.*, pp. 405–7: Vallera is said to place her charms above those of all others "in an attempt to seduce her"; "after having spoken to Nencia of the red stones of the necklace he wishes to give her," he "promises her little ornaments chosen to highlight her charms."

62. Bontempelli, *Il Poliziano*, p. 250.

63. Di San Giusto considers it evident that Lorenzo is writing a caricature of amorous poetry and of the exaggerated praises of the lady who is celebrated in the poem (*La vita*, p. 143).

64. E. Carrara, *La poesia pastorale* (Milan, n.d.), p. 226.

65. De Robertis includes among Lorenzo's achievements having translated the eclogue into popular and rustic forms ("L'esperienza," p. 494).

Chapter Four

1. *Scritti scelti di Lorenzo de'Medici*, ed. E. Bigi, p. 241.

2. A. Rochon, *La jeunesse de Laurent de Médicis*, p. 139; see his study of the evidence for dating the various poems, pp. 140–46. Also see D. De Robertis, "L'esperienza poetica del Quattrocento," p. 495.

3. *Scritti scelti*, ed. Bigi, p. 241, and Bigi's "Lorenzo lirico," pp. 241–44.

4. See De Robertis, "L'esperienza," and Chapter 2 of this volume.

5. For an example of this type of sterile imitation in the *Rime*, see sonnet 39: "I am so certain, Love, of your uncertainty." See also Rochon, *La jeunesse*, pp. 153–54.

6. De Robertis, "L'esperienza poetica," p. 496.

7. The other sonnets on the theme of the gift of violets are *Rime* 72 and 76; see the *Scritti scelti*, ed. Bigi, p. 367, for other treatments.

8. See, for example, A. Garsia, *Il Magnifico e la rinascita*, p. 104, for criticism and examples of this type of imitation.

9. See De Robertis, "L'esperienza poetica," pp. 500–502.

10. The Duke of Calabria is identified as Alfonso of Aragon, who visited Florence in 1467–68, the period in which the sonnet may have been composed. See the *Scritti scelti*, ed. Bigi, p. 261. Rochon gives some examples of the popularity of this type of lament in *La jeunesse*, p. 187, n. 206.

11. See, for example, B. Cicognani's statement of the intensely personal sentiment which runs through the whole *Canzoniere* (*La poesia di Lorenzo de'Medici*, p. 25).

12. Cited in U. Dorini, *Lorenzo dei Medici detto il Magnifico*, p. 253.

13. M. Martelli, *Studi Laurenziani* (Florence, 1965), pp. 107–8. Martelli devotes a chapter to "L'avventurosa storia del 'Comento,'" pp. 51–133.

14. See *Scritti scelti*, ed. Bigi, p. 295, and Rochon, *La jeunesse*, pp. 140–41.

15. Martelli, *Studi*, pp. 124, 71, 106, 133.

16. Garsia, *Il Magnifico*, pp. 85–86.

17. In this definition and in much of the theoretical discussion that follows, Lorenzo bases his argument on Marsilio Ficino's treatise on love, *Sopra lo Amore*; see Bigi's edition of *Scritti scelti*, p. 300, n. 3.

18. In this defense of love as "natural" Lorenzo is not giving rein to "his good sense as a modern man," as Garsia suggests in *Il Magnifico*, p. 87; here again he follows Ficino (*Scritti scelti*, ed. Bigi, p. 303, n. 6).

19. The sonnet is the most worthy form, he asserts, because its brevity presents the greatest difficulty; this defense is clearly an answer to Dante's assertion of the superiority of the *canzone* in *De Vulgari Eloquentia*, II. While not suggesting that his own poems attain the perfection of which the form is capable, Lorenzo considers the attempt itself worthy of praise.

20. Martelli asserts that from 1490 the climate of opinion in Florence was changing, and would soon become unbearable for Lorenzo (*Studi*, pp. 130–31).

21. A. Momigliano, "La poesia del Magnifico," in *Ultimi Studi* (Florence, 1954), p. 111.

22. A. Lipari, *The Dolce Stil Novo according to Lorenzo de'Medici*.

23. See the review of Lipari's book by A. Caraccio, "Laurent de Médicis interprète et continuateur du 'Dolce stil nuovo'?" *Revue des études italiennes*, 3 (1938), 115–25, esp. p. 122: "one will freely admit that the old ideal of the *stil nuovo* merges imperceptibly with the ideal of the Renaissance, but will be reticent when the critic attempts to represent by the features of a lady the mystical death

of early Italian literature, or when he considers this early literature as a true divinity to which one must pray for a new inspiration."

24. For details of this identification, see the *Scritti scelti*, ed. Bigi, p. 313, n. 4.

25. This statement in fact corresponds to the events; a number of other Florentine poets, among them Poliziano, wrote verses lamenting her death.

26. Garsia, for example, says that from this he derives "a poetry lacking in spontaneity . . . which has to look outside itself for both life and form" (*Il Magnifico*, p. 96).

27. *Scritti scelti*, ed. Bigi, p. 295. This is particularly evident in the star-sun metaphor which Lorenzo uses to illustrate the relation of the two experiences: the dead girl had been as a star, and by regarding it he had accustomed his eyes to heavenly light, so that when the sun appeared, eclipsing the star, he was better able to bear its splendor (*Comento*, 330). For Lucrezia Donati, see the *Scritti scelti*, ed. Bigi, pp. 241–42; Rochon, *La jeunesse*, pp. 146-49; and for a detailed study, see I. Del Lungo, *Gli amori del Magnifico Lorenzo* (Bologna, 1923). Rochon points out that Lorenzo follows a long literary tradition in concealing the name of his lady or in referring to her through more or less transparent allusions (p. 167, n. 61).

28. For the texts of the four poems and a brief discussion, see I. Del Lungo, "La tenzone poetica di Amore e Fortuna," in *Florentia. Uomini e cose del Quattrocento* (Florence, 1897).

29. For an examination of these influences, see Garsia, *Il Magnifico*, pp. 99–104, and Rochon, *La jeunesse*, pp. 150–53.

30. See Caraccio's review of Lipari, "Laurent de Médicis," pp. 120–21.

31. N. Scarano demonstrates that Lorenzo is both more and less Platonic than his predecessors, particularly Petrarch, in "Il platonismo nelle poesie di Lorenzo de'Medici," in *Nuova Antologia*, 47 (1893), series III, 49–66.

32. Garsia terms this "the earthly finality of love," "the natural and almost necessary finality of being returned" (*Il Magnifico*, p. 112).

33. *Scritti scelti*, ed. Bigi, p. 296.

34. G. Thomas in his *Etude sur l'expression de l'amour platonique dans la pœésie italienne du moyen âge et de la renaissance* (Paris, 1892) overstates Lorenzo's originality in asserting that he "determines theoretically the Italian doctrine of platonic love" for his period (p. 51). Lorenzo's influence is rather on the poetic expression of this theory.

35. Martelli, *Studi*, p. 74; for a brief survey of the philosophy of love in the period, see pp. 73–75.

36. *Ibid.*, p. 74. Martelli cites as example of an extreme use of this analysis the commentary by Pico della Mirandola to a *canzone* by Girolamo Benivieni, in which six stages of the scale of love are distinguished.

37. For the tendency to stress the prose values of the poetry itself, see De Robertis, "L'esperienza," pp. 496, 503.

38. R. Spongano in *Un capitolo di storia della nostra prosa d'arte* (Florence, 1941) praises Lorenzo along with Alberti and Sannazzaro as the only vernacular prose writers of the period whose works reveal a careful study of form and a knowledgeable stylistic ideal (p. 27). For the discussion of Lorenzo's prose in particular, see pp. 34–38.

39. Fubini, *Studi sulla letteratura del Rinascimento*, p. 129. He cites numerous examples of these stylistic tendencies, particularly on pp. 130, 134–35.

40. *Ibid.*, p. 136.

41. E. M. Fusco, *La lirica*, 175.

Chapter Five

1. References to the text are to A. Simioni's edition, *Opere di Lorenzo de'Medici*, II.

2. For a discussion of the evolution of the *ballata* form, see M. Bowra, "Songs of Dance and Carnival," in *Italian Renaissance Studies: A Tribute to the late Cecilia M. Ady* (London, 1960), especially pp. 328–32.

3. *Ibid.*, p. 331.

4. *Ibid.*, p. 332.

5. A. Momigliano in his chapter on the *canti carnascialeschi* in *Studi di Poesia* (Bari, 1948), pp. 57–63, discusses the peculiarly Florentine nature of both the *canzoni a ballo* and the *canti*, and J.-P. Barricelli considers the *canti* within the context of the Florentine cultural tradition in "Revisiting the *Canti Carnascialeschi*," *Italian Quarterly*, 43 (1967), 43–61. Barricelli finds in these songs "a profound cultural expression of an artistic people, a kind of popular *epos*" (p. 59).

6. For a discussion of the different emphasis which both Lorenzo and Poliziano give to the courtly ideal, see Bowra, "Songs of Dance and Carnival," p. 334.

7. The translation of these verses is that of J. Tusiani in *Italian Poets of the Renaissance* (Long Island City, N. Y., 1971), pp. 68–69.

8. See the *Scritti scelti di Lorenzo de'Medici*, ed. E. Bigi, p. 209.

9. Cited in *Scritti scelti*, ed. Bigi, pp. 231–32.

10. The poem is translated by Tusiani, *Italian Poets*, pp. 72–73.

11. See, for example, Bowra, "Songs of Dance and Carnival," pp. 345–46.

12. *Ibid.*, p. 335.

13. *Ibid.*, p. 352.

14. See M. Martelli's chapter, "Una vacanza letteraria di Lorenzo: il Carnevale di 1490" in *Studi laurenziani*, pp. 37–49.

15. *Lorenzo de'Medici, Scritti scelti*, ed. E. Bellorini (Turin, 1927), p. 17.

16. Tusiani translates the poem in *Italian Poets*, pp. 70–71.

17. Tusiani's translation of "Fate will always have its way" for this verse suggests a meaning rather different from Lorenzo's words.

18. A. Loria, "La poesia di Lorenzo il Magnifico," in *Libera cattedra di storia della civiltà fiorentina: Il Quattrocento* (Florence, 1954), p. 89.

19. A. Momigliano, "La poesia del Magnifico," in *Ultimi studi*, p. 107.

20. Bowra, "Songs of Dance and Carnival," p. 334.

21. P. O. Kristeller, "Lorenzo de'Medici platonico," *Giornale critico della filosofia italiana*, 29 (1938), 149–53.

22. R. Palmarocchi, "Studi e ricerche sulla vita di Lorenzo il Magnifico: il problema dell'autografia," *Archivio storico italiano*, 14 (1930), 286.

23. The edition of the *novelle* cited is that of Del Lungo in *Gli amori del Magnifico Lorenzo* (Giacoppo, pp. 111–23; Ginevra, pp. 124–38). In his introduction to the *novelle*, Del Lungo presents the circumstances of their first publication and subsequent identification. See also Palmarocchi, "Studi e ricerche." The identification was not immediately universally accepted; G. Fatini, for example, editing the *Novelle del Quattrocento* (Turin, 1944), said that the author of the *Giacoppo* could not be identified.

24. Fatini, *Novelle*, pp. 167, 177.

25. Lorenzo's defense of the lady's conduct is on pp. 112-13 of Del Lungo's edition.

26. Fatini, *Novelle*, p. 176.

27. Fatini points out that the "infernal cleverness" of the ruse lies in the fact that "its execution is entrusted entirely to its victim" (*ibid.*, p. 180).

28. Comparing the two *frati* on several counts, Fatini prefers Machiavelli's characterization as more natural (*ibid.*, pp. 174–75).

29. *Ibid.*, p. 168.

30. Palmarocchi, "Studi e ricerche," p. 286, n. 1.

31. V. Rossi, for example, compares Lorenzo favorably with the

famed writer of *novelle*, Luigi Pulci, in *Il Quattrocento, Storia letteraria d'Italia*, V, pp. 207–8.

Chapter Six

1. *Scritti scelti di Lorenzo de'Medici*, ed. E. Bigi, p. 453.
2. See, for example, D. De Robertis, "L'esperienza," p. 505; see also *Scritti scelti*, ed. Bigi, p. 495, and U. Dorini, *Lorenzo dei Medici detto il Magnifico* p. 264.
3. De Robertis, "L'esperienza," p. 505.
4. The generally accepted period of its composition is not long before 1486, when the poem is mentioned in Poliziano's *Nutricia*. See the Bigi edition of *Scritti scelti*, p. 453. M. Martelli's recent hypothesis is that the poem, retouched by Lorenzo after 1486, was composed in its original form at a much earlier date, probably in 1464; see his introduction to the *Opere* of Lorenzo (Turin, 1965), I, xiv.
5. The descriptive style is similar to that of Dante. Specifically, compare *Inferno*, II, 1–5, with the opening two stanzas of *Corinto*.
6. An early and detailed study is that of A. Simioni, *La materia e le fonti del "Corinto"* (Perugia, 1904). See also the more recent study of B. Maier, *Lettura critica del "Corinto" di Lorenzo de'Medici* (Trieste, 1949), p. 17.
7. B. Maier, *Lettura critica*, p. 13.
8. See Dorini, *Lorenzo*, p. 271.
9. See De Robertis, "L'esperienza," pp. 505–6. Several critics have called attention to this successful accommodation of the classical and the modern; see, for example, Dorini, *Lorenzo*, p. 271, and V. Rossi, *Il Quattrocento: Storia letteraria d'Italia*, V, p. 340, who observes that the fresh air of the Tuscan countryside dissipates the stale aura of the schools in the use of these classical sources.
10. B. Maier, *Lettura critica*, p. 21.
11. *Ibid.*, p. 48.
12. *Ibid.*, p. 44.
13. *Ibid.*, for example, p. 54.
14. See especially *Inferno*, XIV, 97–99.
15. Editors of the poem frequently consider this invocation to the nymph, consisting of some twenty verses, to be the song of Apollo. Bigi, however, follows Del Lungo in observing that the poet is calling upon his own lady, to hear his own song and to inspire him in presenting the divine verses of the gods; see the Bigi edition, *Scritti scelti*, p. 458.
16. *Ibid.*, p. 453. De Robertis states that the eclogue merely runs

through the entire idyllic, mythological, and rhetorical repertory of the type ("L'esperienza," p. 505).

17. See N. Spagnolo, *Apollo e Pan, carme bucolico di Lorenzo de'Medici* (Cremona, 1930) and its review in *Giornale storico della letteratura italiana*, 97 (1931), 199 ff.

18. Verses 94–96 and 165–66; see the Bigi edition of *Scritti scelti*, p. 458, note to v. 94, and p. 461, notes to vv. 165–66, 173–75.

19. A. Garsia, *Il Magnifico e la rinascita*, p. 171.

20. *Ibid.*, p. 170.

21. *Ibid.*, p. 159.

22. De Robertis, "L'esperienza," p. 505.

23. Rochon, *La jeunesse de Laurent de Médicis*, p. 262. For a listing of other poems referring to the villa, see his n. 236, p. 287.

24. For the story of Arethusa, see Ovid's *Metamorphoses*, V, trans. R. Humphries (Bloomington and London, 1968), pp. 125–27. E. L. S. Horsburgh published an illustration of an engraving of the story of Ambra and Ombrone cut in relief in an amber flask which belonged to Lorenzo, and commented that the suggestion for the poem may have come from this flask (*Lorenzo the Magnificent and Florence in her Golden Age*, p. 398).

25. C. Stange illustrates the extensive influence of Dante's ninth *canzone* in the descriptions of nature in the *Ambra*; see the notes to his presentation of the poem, *Lorenzo il Magnifico*, I, 190–91.

26. The "gentle flower" grown up "in its lap" and characterized by "honor, wealth, and empire" is apparently Florence; see Stange, *Lorenzo*, I, 191.

27. The quotation is from Humphries's translation, p. 125.

28. A. Capasso insists that Ombrone is either a river, and thus cannot burn, or, instead, the god of a river, and can "burn" with emotion like any other god (*Tre saggi sulla poesia italiana del Rinascimento*, p. 282); he adds, however, that one finds in very few poets "so live, spontaneous, and profound a sense that great love is a fusion of sensuality and affection, of voluptuousness and tenderness" (*ibid.*, p. 286).

29. See Garsia, *Il Magnifico*, p. 180.

30. S. Brinton, *The Golden Age of the Medici*, p. 187.

31. Capasso, *Tre saggi*, pp. 276, 287.

32. A. Bailly, *La Florence des Médicis* (Paris, 1942), p. 190.

33. See the Bigi edition, *Scritti scelti*, p. 495.

34. Capasso, considering this the best of the poem's components, praises the manner in which the lady's passionate memory of the encounter purifies the element of sensuality, resulting in a highly complex sentiment rich in affectionate gentleness (*Tre saggi*, p. 203).

35. *Ibid.*, p. 266.

36. The title first appeared in a Florentine edition dating perhaps from the end of the fifteenth century: see Bigi's edition of *Scritti scelti*, p. 495.

37. Dorini, *Lorenzo*, p. 264.

38. L. Di San Giusto agrees with Thomas that Lorenzo was affected by "a languor of the spirit, without a determined object," which colors his sorrow for an irreparably lost past, and introduces a note of melancholy even into present happiness (*La vita e l'opera di Lorenzo il Magnifico*, p. 131).

39. This is the generally accepted critical assessment of the poem. G. Flores, for example, declares that both *Selve* are badly constructed, and that even in the more successful segments, such as the descriptions of the Golden Age and the coming of summer, the poetry lacks a center and reduces to an enumeration, its interest in the isolated particular rather than in the work as a whole (in *Storia illustrata della letteratura italiana scritta da un gruppo di studiosi* [1942], I, 337).

40. For a detailed study of Lorenzo's use of his sources, both the classical elements and those drawn from the vernacular Italian tradition, see G. Bottiglioni, "Sulle Selve del Magnifico Lorenzo de'Medici," *Rivista abruzzese*, 26 (1911), 473–87.

41. Capasso, *Tre saggi*, p. 213.

Chapter Seven

1. N. Scarano, "Il platonismo nelle poesie di Lorenzo dei Medici," *Nuova Antologia*, 46 (1893), 623. A. Garsia expresses the same reaction, pointing out that the work's exposition of several philosophical doctrines fills it with so many names that it seems more a school exercise than a work of poetry (*Il Magnifico e la rinascita*, p. 137).

2. F. Bérence suggests that the poem reveals nuances in the poet's character that are particularly important because he is unaware of revealing them (*Laurent le Magnifique ou la quête da la perfection*, p. 141).

3. Here and at many other points in the poem, C. Stange points out echoes of Dante and Petrarch (*Lorenzo il Magnifico*, I, 192). See also the notes to A. Rochon's chapter on the *Altercazione* (*La jeunesse de Laurent de Médicis*, pp. 515–43) for sources and comparisons.

4. As noted by Stange, Marsilio here refutes the ideal of the Stoics and the Cynics; Dante, too, had discussed Zeno and the Stoics in his *Convivio* (Stange, *Lorenzo*, I, 193).

5. Stange recalls the description in Plato's *Phaedrus*, used by Landino in the opening section of his *Disputationes Camaldulenses*,

upon which Lorenzo patterned much of his first chapter (*ibid.*, I, 191).

6. See J. B. Wadsworth, "Landino's *Disputationes Camaldulenses,* Ficino's *De Felicitate* and *L'Altercazione* of Lorenzo de'Medici," *Modern Philology,* 50 (1952), 23–31, for a study of the relation between these three texts. This passage is discussed on p. 29.

7. See M. Martelli, *Studi Laurenziani,* p. 26. Rochon, too, stresses the "unquestionable sincerity" of such passages: "The search for a durable tranquillity, opposed to passing and deceptive pleasures, reveals a deep aspiration of his soul" (*La jeunesse,* p. 513).

8. A. Buck, *Der Platonismus in der Dichtungen Lorenzo de'Medici* (Berlin, 1936); the *Altercazione* is discussed as an example of the Platonism *sub specie aeternitatis* treated on pp. 70–108.

9. See Rochon, *La jeunesse,* pp. 510–13. While Rochon considers it "beyond doubt" that Lorenzo's oration "is nothing but an adaptation" of Ficino's work, he acknowledges that there are brief original passages, and that "Lorenzo's work doesn't produce exactly the same sound as that of Ficino" (p. 511). A series of letters on the subject of the proper direction of life, exchanged by Lorenzo and Ficino, is particularly interesting as further evidence of Lorenzo's genuine attempt to find some sort of a solution through philosophy. "Knowing as we do the constancy of Lorenzo's search for peace as a theme which runs through his poetry, we may see here yet another facet of this quest. For a moment, Lorenzo must have hoped that Ficino's doctrine could bring him repose" (J. B. Wadsworth, "Lorenzo de'Medici and Marsilio Ficino: An Experiment in Platonic Friendship," *Romanic Review,* 46 [1955], 95).

10. A version of the first three verses of the oration, in the hand of Lorenzo's chancellor Niccolo Michelozzi, appears on the back of a letter received by Lorenzo in the autumn of 1473. See Martelli, *Studi,* pp. 1–3.

11. *Ibid.*, 11–12, 34–35. Martelli's whole chapter on "Il Guazzabuglio dell'*Altercazione*" examines the problem in detail (pp. 1–35). As evidence of his contention, Martelli cites a letter from Gentile Becchi in 1473; Becchi, now bishop of Arezzo and far from Florence, asks a friend to send him "the three chapters by Lorenzo *On the Supreme Good*"; the *Altercazione,* or its earlier version, is the only one of Lorenzo's works to which this title would apply.

12. See Wadsworth, "Landino's *Disputationes,*" for a summary of the various views. The most important of these belonged to Kristeller, who suggested also that a single draft of the argument, composed in Latin by Ficino, had served as basis both for the *Altercazione* and the *De Felicitate* itself (in his review of Buck's *Platonismus* in *Giornale critico della filosofia italiana*).

13. Wadsworth, "Landino's *Disputationes*," p. 26.

14. *Ibid.*, pp. 28, 31. Martelli disputes Wadsworth's conclusions in detail in *Studi*, pp. 8–13.

15. Martelli, *Studi*, p. 29.

16. Wadsworth, "Landino's *Disputationes*," p. 31.

17. See Rochon, *La jeunesse*, p. 599, for a discussion of the evidence for this order.

18. Bigi in his edition (*Scritti scelti*, p. 91) presents these seven poems without distinction as *capitoli religiosi*, but Rochon usefully distinguishes between the five properly termed *orazioni* and the two others (*La jeunesse*, p. 616, n. 8).

19. See C. Bonardi, "Le orazioni di Lorenzo il Magnifico e l'inno finale della Circe di G. B. Gelli," *Giornale storico della letteratura italiana*, 33 (1899), 77–82, and E. H. Wilkins, "Lorenzo de'Medici and Boethius," *Modern Philology*, 15 (1917), 63–64.

20. For a discussion and analysis of Lorenzo's treatment of these texts, see Rochon, *La jeunesse*, pp. 603–6.

21. *Ibid.*, p. 602.

22. For Ficino's preference and influence in Lorenzo's choice of these texts, see *ibid.*, pp. 600–602. Both Garsia and Buck (*Der Platonismus*) discuss the importance of theism in these works in their appeal to Ficino, to Lorenzo, and to many of their humanist contemporaries.

23. Bigi in his edition notes that the manuscripts present the poem as addressed to Feo Belcari, but cites also a letter from G. B. Salviati stating that the sonnet had been addressed to him by Lorenzo while he was preaching in Florence (*Scritti scelti*, p. 263, n. 26).

24. For the development of the literary *laude* from the popular form, see Garsia, *Il Magnifico*, pp. 147–50. Rossi explains that in reading them, we feel the same sense of melancholy as one who leaves an open field, having breathed deeply of the fragrance of wild flowers, to enter a room where the same types of flowers spread their perfume from a fine porcelain vase (cited in Garsia, *Il Magnifico*, p. 149).

25. *Ibid.*, p. 151.

26. Garsia, for example, maintains that Lorenzo sings with a voice that is loud, resounding, and grave, as if to conceal the absence of inspiration, adding that he does not feel God intimately (*ibid.*, p. 143).

27. For a discussion of the *sacra rappresentazione* as it developed in Florence, see A. D'Ancona, *Sacre Rappresentazioni* (Florence, 1877).

28. J. S. Kennard, *The Italian Theatre from its Beginnings to the Close of the Seventeenth Century* (New York, 1932), p. 37.
29. K. Hillebrand, "La politique dans le mystère du XVe siècle," p. 204.
30. Kennard, *Italian Theatre*, pp. 41–42.
31. See A. D'Ancona, *Origini del teatro italiano* (2d ed., Turin, 1891), pp. 255–57, 259–61.
32. D'Ancona and more recently A. Chiari in "Prospettive Laurenziane," in *Indagini e letture*, I (Florence, 1954), accept 1489. The later date of February 1491 is accepted by H. A. Matthes, "On the date of Lorenzo's *Sacra Rappresentazione di S. Giovanni e Paolo*," *Aevum*, 25 (1951), 324–28; by S. Della Palma, "Prologo alla sacra rappresentazione del Magnifico," *Aevum*, 36 (1962), 430–42; and by De Robertis, "L'esperienza poetica," p. 510.
33. F. Bérence, *Laurent le magnifique ou la quête de la perfection*, p. 279.
34. *Scritti scelti*, ed. Bigi, p. 6.
35. For this type of critique, see, for example, Hillebrand, "La politique," pp. 222–23.
36. A. Chiari, "Costantino, Giuliano e Lorenzo de'Medici," in *Il mondo nel rinascimento; Atti del V convegno internazionale di studi sul rinascimento* (Florence, 1958), pp. 75–92.
37. Hillebrand, "La politique," p. 223.
38. Kennard, *Italian Theatre*, p. 37.
39. Bérence, *Laurent*, p. 278.
40. Chiari, "Costantino," pp. 85–86.
41. See, for example, Hillebrand, "La politique," p. 229, and Bérence, *Laurent*, p. 279.
42. Chiari, "Costantino," p. 89.
43. Garsia, *Il Magnifico*, pp. 164–65, 168–69.
44. A. Loria, "La poesia di Lorenzo il Magnifico," p. 85.

Conclusion

1. A review of recent major studies is found in R. Starn, "Florentine Renaissance Studies," *Bibliothèque d'Humanisme et Renaissance*, 32 (1970), 677–84. For an account of studies of Lorenzo's work, see B. Maier in *I classici italiani nella storia della critica*.
2. For an interesting study of one aspect of this effort, see E. Garin, "La letteratura degli umanisti," in *Storia della letteratura italiana*, III (Milan, 1966).
3. It is significant that his basic aim has frequently been described in terms which are abstract and philosophical, not literary. A. Bailly claims that the essential need and aspiration which unifies his

personality is "the pursuit and possession of beauty" (*La Florence des Médicis* [Paris, 1942]), p. 181. Bérence devotes his volume to Lorenzo's "quest for perfection" (*Laurent le Magnifique ou la quête de la perfection*).

4. See, for example, Rochon, "A l'ombre du laurier," pp. 76–77.

5. See B. Maier in *I classici italiani nella storia della critica*, p. 330, and his *Problemi ed esperienze di critica letteraria* (Siena, 1950), pp. 31–32.

Selected Bibliography

PRIMARY SOURCES

Scritti scelti. Edited by E. Bellorini. Turin: UTET, 1927.
Scritti scelti di Lorenzo de'Medici. Edited by E. Bigi. 2nd ed. Turin: UTET, 1965.
Opere di Lorenzo de'Medici. Edited by A. Simioni, 2d ed., 2 vols. Bari: Laterza, 1939. The Simioni edition contains no critical comment; information on the manuscripts and establishment of texts is found in Vol. II.
Il Poliziano, il Magnifico, lirici del Quattrocento. Anthology and commentary by M. Bontempelli. Florence: Sansoni, 1910; new ed. by G. Ghinassi, 1969. The comments preceding the selections are brief but frequently useful, including reference to major critical views.
Lorenzo de'Medici, Opere. Edited by M. Martelli. Turin: Caula, 1965. Particularly important for the discussion of chronology and of the elaboration of the works. See also Martelli's excellent separate edition of the *Simposio.* Florence: Olschki, 1966.

SECONDARY SOURCES

ADY, C. M. *Lorenzo dei Medici and Renaissance Italy.* New York: Collier Books, 1966. Considers Lorenzo as a child of his period in this "study of the humanistic ideals and the harsh realities of Italy's Golden Age."
BARFUCCI, E. *Lorenzo il Magnifico e la società artistica del suo tempo.* 2d ed. Florence: Gonnelli, 1964. A detailed study of artistic achievements related to Lorenzo's patronage, which the author considers sincere, motivated primarily by a genuine love of beauty.
BARON, H. *The Crisis of the Early Italian Renaissance.* Rev. ed. Princeton: Princeton University Press, 1966. A one-volume edition of Baron's major work, particularly important to students of the Florentine Renaissance for its treatment of the humanists and of "the interplay of ideas and events."
BÉRENCE, F. *Laurent le Magnifique ou la quête de la perfection.* Paris: La Colombe, 1949. Very sympathetic to Lorenzo and the tradi-

tions of which he is a part; asserts the attempt to reconcile the
active and contemplative as a key to Lorenzo's activity throughout his life.

BIGI, E. "Lorenzo lirico," pp. 23–45, in *Dal Petrarca al Leopardi,
studi di stilistica storica*. Milan-Naples: Ricciardi, 1954. Studies
the successive stages of Lorenzo's poetic development and discusses chronology.

BIZZARRI, E. *Il Magnifico Lorenzo*. Milan: Mondadori, 1950. Relates
Lorenzo's achievements to a desire for self-affirmation; emphasizes the variety of his activities and the serious nature of his
accomplishment.

BRINTON, S. *The Golden Age of the Medici*. London: Methuen, 1931.
Treats the period 1434-1494: Cosimo, Piero, and Lorenzo.

CAPASSO, A. *Tre saggi sulla poesia italiana del rinascimento*. Genoa:
Emiliano degli Orfini, 1939. Treats the major tendencies in
Lorenzo's poetry; excellent commentary on individual works.

CHIARI, A. "Prospettive Laurenziane," in *Indagini e letture*, vol. I.
Florence: Le Monnier, 1966. Comments on the change in critical
attitudes to Lorenzo and his poetry and on a number of specific
questions raised by the study of both.

CICOGNANI, B. *La poesia di Lorenzo de'Medici*. Florence: Le Monnier,
1950. Denies the accusation that Lorenzo was "corrupt and a
corruptor," and studies his poetry as a direct reflection of the
man, "the history of his soul."

DE ROBERTIS, D. "L'esperienza poetica del Quattrocento," in *Storia
della letteratura italiana*. Vol. 3. Milan: Garzanti, 1966. De
Robertis devotes a chapter to the "Age of Lorenzo," with
valuable commentary on the works of Lorenzo's contemporaries
and on his position with relation to them.

DORINI, U. *Lorenzo dei Medici detto il Magnifico*. Florence: Vallecchi,
1949. Asserts poetry as Lorenzo's "natural vocation," the cult
of the beautiful in all its manifestations.

Florence au temps de Laurent le Magnifique. Collection "Ages d'Or
et Réalités." Paris: Hachette, 1965. In addition to A. Rochon's
essay "A l'ombre du Laurier," the handsome volume contains
useful chapters on the city, the Medici bank, and numerous
illustrations from the art of the period.

GAGE, J. *Life in Italy at the Time of the Medici*. New York: Capri-
corn Books, 1970. A social history, offering a correction to
Burckhardt's interpretation of Renaissance Italy.

HORSBURGH, E. L. S. *Lorenzo the Magnificent and Florence in her
Golden Age*. London: Methuen, 1908. Praises in particular
Lorenzo's contribution to narrowing the literary distance between

the erudite and the unlearned, through his own work and through his encouragement of vernacular writing.

LIPARI, A. *The Dolce Stil Novo according to Lorenzo de'Medici.* New Haven: Yale University Press, 1936. Sees in the first part of the *Comento* a treatise on love according to the *dolce stil nuovo*, and discusses the relation of Lorenzo's work to that tradition, particularly to Dante's *Vita Nuova* and *Convivio*.

LORIA, A. "La poesia di Lorenzo il Magnifico," pp. 70–92, in *Libera Cattedra di storia della civiltà fiorentina*. Florence: Sansoni, 1954. Lorenzo's poetic works are seen as progressively more individual and less traditional.

MAIER, B. "Lorenzo de'Medici," in *I classici italiani nella storia della critica*, vol. I. Edited by W. Binni. Florence: La Nuova Italia, 1954. Details and illustrates the various approaches to Lorenzo's poetry from his own period to the twentieth century.

MARTELLI, M. *Studi Laurenziani*. Florence: Olschki, 1965. Concerned primarily with the establishment of a chronology for several of Lorenzo's poems, through a detailed study of letters and other documents of the period. Martelli's conclusions have not been universally accepted, but the study is of fundamental importance.

MOMIGLIANO, A. "La poesia del Magnifico," pp. 107–12, in *Ultimi Studi*. Florence: La Nuova Italia, 1954. Explains the "disconcerting variety" of Lorenzo's poetry by assertion of two contrary tendencies, that toward observation and realism and that toward meditation and melancholy, which alternate but do not intimately combine.

MONNIER, P. *Le Quattrocento*. Paris: Perrin, 1912. Detailed and still useful. In addition to the chapter on Lorenzo's court (II, 22–74), other chapters on the cultural and intellectual movements of the period are valuable for understanding of the context of Lorenzo's literary contribution.

PALMAROCCHI, R. *Lorenzo il Magnifico*. Turin: UTET, reprinted 1946. Studies Lorenzo himself as the necessary condition for understanding both his public life and his work; sees in him a perfect unity of medieval and Renaissance characteristics; a very favorable interpretation.

PANCRAZI, P. *Nel Giardino di Candido*. Florence: Vallecchi, 1950. Contains a chapter on the "attraction" of Lorenzo, the recent tendency to consider him no longer a Renaissance enigma but a modern ruler, and the contrary interpretations of all aspects of his activity.

ROCHON, A. *La jeunesse de Laurent de Médicis*. Paris: Les Belles Lettres, 1963. Author covers the period from 1449 to 1478, the year of the Pazzi conspiracy. Attempts a complete image of Lorenzo, refusing arbitrary separation of his literary work from his political life and his activity as patron. Very extensive documentation, comments on previous critical evaluations, interesting presentation and frequently very informative notes. The most useful book on this period of Lorenzo's life and his early works.

Rossi, V. *Il Quattrocento*, in *Storia letteraria d'Italia*, V. 3d ed., Milan: Vallardi, 1945. For Lorenzo's literary role, see pp. 336–52 on Rome and Florence during his period.

Rubenstein, N., ed. *Florentine Studies: Politics and Society in Renaissance Florence*. London: Faber and Faber, 1968. Because of studies such as these, as R. Starn points out in his detailed review of this volume in *Bibl. d'Hum. et Ren.*, 32 (1970), 77–84, "the Quattrocento looks very different than it did a generation ago." A major contribution and reorientation.

Stange, C. *Lorenzo il Magnifico*. 2 vols. Bremen: Hauschild, 1940. Particularly interesting is the discussion of three periods in Lorenzo's poetry, in vol. II, chap. 2, "Eros und Agape."

Index

DATE DUE
